To the memory of Anne van Meeuwen (1950–2001), a much valued and respected colleague.

Notes on contributors

Andrea de Berker manages Barnardo's Hamara Family Project, a short breaks project in partnership with the London Borough of Waltham Forest, and has done so for the past 12 years.

Alan Coombe is a Principal Officer, Policy and Practice and leads on the area of Family life in Barnardo's.

Katherine Curtis worked for one year with Barnardo's as a Research Assistant and is now a Research Assistant at City University in London.

Angie Gillies worked with Barnardo's Scotland as a senior practitioner for six years, first at Watling Lodge and then Family Placement Services. She took up a post with NCH in April 2000, in a new scheme providing fostering placements to teenagers as an alternative to custody.

Christine Lenehan was the Project Leader of Families Together, a Barnardo's short breaks project, for over ten years. She is now working as Principal Officer for the Council for Disabled Children.

Sue MacFadyen has worked in Barnardo's Family Placement Services for over 12 years and before that in residential child care. Her special interest is in long-term support issues in adoption.

Nellie Maan is the manager of the Barnardo's Better Play project. Prior to that she managed the Khandaani Dhek Bhal project in Yorkshire, and has worked for Barnardo's since 1996.

Jan Morrison has been a Project Leader at Barnardo's for the past eight years and is currently managing Family Link, a short breaks project in partnership with the London Borough of Newham.

Tony Newman is a Principal Officer, Research and Development at Barnardo's. He has worked for the organisation since 1990 and has particular responsibility for work in the area of health and disability.

Satnam Singh has worked in Barnardo's Family Placement Services for over seven years and has taken the lead role in developing services for black children through the Khandan Initiative.

Are we listening yet?

working with minority ethnic
communities – some models of practice

edited by Darshan Sachdev and Anne van Meeuwen

LEARNING RESOURCES
CENTRE
Havering College
of Further and Higher education

39098

362.84
Q

Barnardo's
GIVING CHILDREN BACK THEIR FUTURE

Barnardo's vision is that the lives of all children and young people should be free from poverty, abuse and discrimination.

Barnardo's purpose is to help the most vulnerable children and young people transform their lives and fulfil their potential.

© Barnardo's

All rights reserved. This publication may not be reproduced, stored on a retrieval system, or transmitted in any form or by any means without prior permission of the publisher.

First published in 2002 by Barnardo's

Tanners Lane
Barkingside
Ilford
Essex IG6 IQG

Charity registration number 216250

A catalogue record for this book is available from the British Library

ISBN 0 902046 78 0

Notes on editors

Darshan Sachdev was a Principal Officer, Research and Development at Barnardo's from 1995 to 2000, where she had lead responsibility for education. She worked with minority ethnic communities for over six years before joining Barnardo's. She is now Evaluation and Analysis Manager for the Lambeth, Southwark and Lewisham Health Action Zone.

Anne van Meeuwen was a Principal Officer, Policy and Practice at Barnardo's, leading in the area of adoption and fostering, and keeping children safe. Prior to joining Barnardo's in 1994, she worked for 15 years as a social work manager in a local authority with a high proportion of families from minority ethnic communities. Anne died suddenly, shortly before the publication of this book, and is sadly missed by colleagues at Barnardo's.

Contents

Acknowledgements

We would like to express our grateful thanks to Kristin Liabo for her invaluable help with checking the references, and to our library colleagues for their patient and unstinting support with literature searches and locating hard-to-find references. Thanks are also due to Grace Mason, Yvonne Huddart, Judy Allan and Vicky Harris for their generous help with word-processing the amendments to various drafts of the manuscript, and to Sylvia Potter for copy-editing it.

We would also like to record our gratitude to Dr Ravinder Barn, who gave invaluable advice and suggestions on the whole manuscript.

Darshan Sachdev and Ann van Meeuwen

Foreword

'There was not one other door in all London that would open to him, save the workhouse alone' (Dr Barnardo's Homes, Annual Report, 1890:78)

Barnardo's commitment to providing a service to all the members of an ethnically diverse community can be traced back to this reference found in Barnardo's archives, of the support offered to a young 18-year-old from the Caribbean. Claudius Tiberius Alexandrinus arrived in Liverpool on a ship, which then discharged him and left him to fend for himself. Lacking a livelihood or any other means with which to feed and protect himself against the inclement weather, Claudius eventually made his way to London. Once there and looking for shelter at a lodging house, he was directed to Stepney Causeway, one of the first Barnardo's Homes, since it was well known, as Dr Barnardo wrote, that 'he would not knock in vain at my door' (p78).

The organisation founded by Thomas Barnardo with the aim of helping children and young people whom nobody could or would help, is now, at the beginning of the 21st Century, the largest voluntary child care organisation in the UK. Its 300 plus major services work with over 50,000 children and young people. Some of these services focus exclusively on work with black and minority ethnic communities, where members of those communities face acute disadvantage which impacts on their family or community life, health, safety, educational attainment, and their ability to participate and be active citizens.

The organisation is committed to providing services that are appropriate and sensitive to the needs of the people who use them. As a voluntary organisation which must be seen to be making a positive difference to the lives of the people with whom it works, if it is to retain the confidence of its funders and donors, it is uniquely placed to encourage and foster creativity and innovation in practice. One of the factors which ensures the continuation of funding from various sources is user satisfaction with services received. For users from an ethnically diverse community, this can only be achieved if the organisation values differences and caters for those differences in appropriate ways. As Darshan Sachdev notes in her introduction to this collection, 'although it is not claimed that Barnardo's has developed "best practice" in all its work with black and minority ethnic communities, it can justifiably be regarded as an organisation with a useful contribution to make'. Our commitment to developing user-responsive services; to evaluating our practice to gauge its effectiveness; the extensive and diverse nature of our services; the UK-wide perspective; and the considerable experience accumulated over the organisation's 130-year-old history – these are some of the factors which have encouraged this collection of some models of practice. The models have been developed by professionals working in partnership with children, young people, parents and carers from minority ethnic communities.

As an organisation which seeks to both learn from our experience and to share that learning internally and externally, we have tried to extract some of the lessons which may be relevant to practice in a variety of contexts. Key themes from the models described are respect, commitment and flexibility, trust and above all, listening. Workers have tried to start from where people are and to hear what they have to say about their situation, their needs and about what services they would find helpful. For generations, children and families from black and minority ethnic communities have experienced not being listened to and of being offered services which others have determined, albeit with the best of intentions, to be appropriate for their needs. We do not believe that we have any cause for complacency but if we ask ourselves the question 'Are we listening yet?' then maybe we can answer that at least in some of our work, the listening has begun.

Roger Singleton CBE
Chief Executive, Barnardo's

1 Introduction

Darshan Sachdev

BARNARDO'S AND ITS WORK WITH MINORITY ETHNIC COMMUNITIES

In 1966, a working party was set up to report on the 'position with regard to children of non-European descent in Dr Barnardo's, whether in residential care or otherwise; to examine the problems arising and to make recommendations'. (Barnardo's, Working Party on Racial Integration, 1966: p13). The report referred to 'coloured' children (the term used by the working party was that prevalent at the time) where one or both parents were not of European descent. Records of children in the care of Dr Barnardo's were examined from 1955, when 515 'fully or partly coloured' children below school leaving age – 7.73% of the total – were in the care of Barnardo's or were receiving family support. Ten years later, the percentage had increased to 20%. This increase was attributed to dual-heritage children of English mothers and Black American servicemen, born during and after the Second World War, and the children of immigrant families from Commonwealth countries.

The working party regarded 'colour' to be a factor which was 'related to certain special child care needs and problems', while asserting that all children had certain basic needs and that 'basic principles of good child care' (p4) applied equally to all children. Of the 70 recommendations made by the working party on developing the work of the organisation with children from minority ethnic communities, one directed staff dealing with 'immigrants' to familiarise themselves with their culture and way of life. Other recommendations included avoiding being influenced by the racially prejudiced views of financial supporters; evaluating the outcomes of the work undertaken with 'coloured' children; and considering inviting universities and trusts to undertake such research (p40).

Barnardo's today is one of the largest voluntary child-care organisations in the UK. Its services provide a range of support to over 50,000 children and families. The number of children, young people and families receiving social care or educational support from Barnardo's services is, however, not a constant. Furthermore, Barnardo's is in the midst of refining and developing its data recording procedures on ethnicity. Therefore, it is not possible at this point in time to provide exact numbers of service users from minority ethnic communities, and estimates only can be given. At the time of writing, we estimate that around 20 per cent of the total number of children, young people and families accessing Barnardo's services throughout UK are from Black and Asian communities (which includes people of Indian, Pakistani, Bangladeshi, Chinese, African or Caribbean origin).

Since the 1966 report, which scrutinised Barnardo's service provision to users from minority ethnic communities, each of Barnardo's eight regions and nations (five regions in England and the three nations of Northern Ireland, Scotland and Wales) has undertaken research and strategic policy work to inform and modify its practice to ensure responsiveness to the needs of its minority ethnic service users. Examples of policy/strategy documents include: Race Equality Strategy for South Wales/South West England (1990); Race Equality Strategy for Scotland (1995); and Race Equality Standards and Strategy (1997) for Barnardo's children's services throughout UK. Some of the recent research projects undertaken by Barnardo's staff or commissioned by Barnardo's have included evaluation of services provided to minority ethnic children, young people and their families in Barnardo's Midlands region (Caesar et al. 1993); a study into the effects of racism on service provision to minority ethnic families in Northern Ireland (Mann-Kler, 1997); a survey of service provision by Scottish Local Authorities and voluntary organisations to minority ethnic children in Scotland (Singh and Patel, 1998); and a qualitative study of South Asian young carers in the Midlands and Yorkshire (Shah and Hatton, 1999).

To counter disadvantage faced by individuals, families and communities, Barnardo's is committed to developing and delivering innovative services that are adequate, appropriate and sensitive to the needs of its users. To ensure that Barnardo's service users from an ethnically diverse population are satisfied with the services they receive, the organisation has to value differences and cater appropriately for those differences. Although it is not claimed that Barnardo's has developed 'best practice' in all its area of work with Black and minority ethnic communities, it can justifiably be regarded as an organisation with a useful contribution to make to the arena of practice development with these communities. In its 130-year history, the organisation has gained valuable practice experience of working with disadvantaged families and communities from diverse ethnic backgrounds. This has been the impetus for this collection of some models of practice in social care provision which have been developed by professionals working in partnership with children, young people and families from minority ethnic communities.

To provide a context for the contributions included in this collection, an historical account of the development of service provision to minority ethnic communities in the United Kingdom is provided, after the rationale for the terminology used in this collection has been considered. A quick glimpse at the legislation introduced in the UK over the last few decades, to effect improvements in service provision to minority ethnic communities, is then followed by a brief review of research undertaken to examine the efficacy and appropriateness of service provision to these communities. This chapter continues with an overview of the five contributions included in this collection, and concludes by pointing a way forward.

TERMINOLOGY

The debates surrounding the terminology which should be adopted to represent minority ethnic communities have been fuelled by ideology and politics, brought into sharp relief by the tension between the opposing needs for political unity *and* a distinct ethnic and/or religious identity. Different terms have their supporters and critics. We are guided by Brown's (1994) advice that:

> *Discussions about terminology with which we feel comfortable have been going on for years and will continue. The use of language to describe individuals or groups is a powerful social tool that can be used to value or to disparage – we need constantly to consider the possible implications of the terms we use and to agree alternatives. To go forward we need to work together, to listen to each other, learn from each other. (p23)*

Hence, rather than enter into the arguments for and against the use of various terms such as Black, Black and Asian or Black and South Asian or minority ethnic communities (those interested in this debate may wish to refer to Dominelli, 1997; Ahmad et al. 1998; Macey, 1995; Modood, 1988, 1994b, 1996), it was decided not to impose terminology on the contributors but to accept terms which they considered to be best suited to the practice, the social context, and the group receiving the service being described. The focus of this collection must remain the practice, and how it can be shaped to be sensitive, adequate and appropriate to its service users rather than on the terminology which is used to describe its recipients.

Our use of the term 'minority ethnic group' reflects that of Yinger's (1976:200) definition:

> *A segment of a larger society whose members are thought, by themselves and/or others, to have a common origin and to share important segments of a common culture and who, in addition, participate in shared activities in which the common origin and culture are significant ingredients.*

SERVICE PROVISION TO MINORITY ETHNIC COMMUNITIES SINCE THE 1950s

Service provision to minority ethnic communities in the United Kingdom has undergone various mutations, shaped in each successive era by the prevailing political ideology emerging in response to the issue of immigration from the Commonwealth countries. From the earliest assimilationist or colour blind perspective to the multicultural perspective, an unchanging outcome has been the failure of the formal welfare sector to meet adequately the needs of minority ethnic communities. The majority of the white voluntary sector has also not escaped criticism for failing to target resources and develop appropriate skills to meet their needs appropriately.

Given that a key objective of social services departments is to deliver services which are accessible, appropriate, adequate and accountable, that is, relevant to the needs of the community in their catchment area (Butt et al. 1994), their failure to do so with regards to minority ethnic communities points towards the fallacies inherent in the ideologies which have underpinned their practice models for those communities.

From assimilation to anti-racism

The assimilationist approach to service provision emerged in the 1950s and 1960s, and reflected the then prevalent model for race relations. It provided a framework within which service provision for minority ethnic communities could be considered. It was underpinned by the belief that immigrant communities would adapt to the norms of the indigenous community and become integrated into the British way of life. Barns (1993) sums up the stance taken by service providers to minority ethnic communities thus:

> Since the ultimate goal was assimilation, the social services did not feel called upon to respond to the specific needs of black people. Indeed, the needs and problems of black people were not even recognized as being different.. (p2-3)

The assimilationist perspective was gradually replaced by a multicultural perspective, or 'cultural pluralism', in the late 1960s and early 1970s. It was founded on the assumption that the needs of the minority ethnic communities were the same as those of white communities, but that the different cultures of the minority communities acted as a barrier to the accessibility of services. This stance had inevitable repercussions for the practice of service providers. Inherent in this perspective is the notion that by overcoming linguistic and cultural barriers which can prevent effective communication and can cause misunderstanding, and by promoting understanding of other cultures, service provision can be made more sensitive and responsive, as it will take into consideration issues of language, diet, religion and culture. It has been argued by several writers, such as Atkin and Rollings (1993), Butt et al. (1994) and Ahmad and Atkin (1996), that such a perspective has severe limitations for service provision to minority ethnic communities.

Firstly, the multicultural perspective encourages the use of generalised summaries of key minority cultural characteristics by service providers. This can lead to an inadequate understanding of minority ethnic cultures, resulting in the reinforcement and perpetuation of cultural stereotypes and myths, such as, 'Asian families look after their own', resulting in neglect by default at best and denial at worst, of the needs of vulnerable members of the Asian community (Atkin and Rollings, 1993).

Secondly, such a perspective, with its emphasis on different cultural practices, leads service providers to blame the minority communities 'for either experiencing specific problems or not making "appropriate" use of services' because of 'their supposedly deviant and unsatisfactory lifestyles' (Ahmad and Atkin, 1996:4). This stance shifts the responsibility for the take-up of services on to minority groups rather than obliging service providers to examine and ensure the relevance of available services for minority communities.

Thirdly, the multicultural perspective, focusing as it does on cultural differences, emphasises the degree of deviation of minority ethnic cultures from the norm of white culture, and has at times engendered a service response from some statutory and voluntary service providers which is centred around the 'special needs' of black and minority ethnic communities. An example would be fostering and adoption where black and minority ethnic children are, by virtue of their ethnic origin, placed in the categories of 'special needs' and 'hard to place'. 'Specialist services' are therefore established to meet the 'special needs' of minority ethnic communities and are used by mainstream providers 'to absolve themselves of the responsibility for ensuring access and appropriateness of services' (Ahmad and Atkin, 1996:3). The development of such services has been financed, in the main, by specific, often time-limited, funding streams, such as, Section 11 funding from the Home Office.

Hence, the multicultural perspective prompted service providers to create specialist services for ethnic minority communities, which led to the marginalisation of the needs of these communities *and* of the services temporarily set up to address these needs (Butt et al. 1994; Ahmad et al. 1998). This perspective, therefore, failed to provide the necessary impetus to service providers to modify the mainstream services to ensure their appropriateness for all members of the local community irrespective of their ethnic background.

Fourthly, it failed to take sufficient account of the structural barriers to access to services encountered by minority ethnic users. When services are organised to white norms, the dietary, linguistic, religious and caring needs of minority ethnic users are often overlooked (Ahmad and Atkin, 1996).

Fifthly, the multicultural perspective, by focusing exclusively on cultural differences, fails to recognise the imbalance in power relationships between the dominant 'white' majority and the minority cultures. Black people's experiences of social services can not simply be attributed to cultural differences, but must be understood as resulting from a confluence of their 'political, social and economic positions', which are 'related to historical legacies of colonialism and post-colonial relationships', argue Ahmad and Atkin (1996:5). They advocate the adoption of an anti-racist perspective which gives due recognition to the structural disadvantage and racism encountered by minority ethnic communities in their interaction with service providers, as reflected in their over-representation in aspects of social services activity which involves overt control and institutionalisation, and under-representation in the receipt of supportive and preventative services (Atkin and Rollings, 1993; Butt et al. 1994; Ahmad and Atkin, 1996).

It would be simplistic to argue that the multicultural perspective has achieved nothing. However, by focusing on the lack of understanding caused by linguistic and cultural barriers, it is limited in what it can achieve as by concentrating on language and cultural differences it does not take into account the impact of racial discrimination, both personal and institutional, on minority communities. Neither does it focus attention on the practice of the service providers, such as social service departments (SSDs) themselves. Butt et al. cogently sum up this position:

> *Ensuring that the services provided by SSDs are culturally and linguistically appropriate is important, but it can only be considered as ensuring that the packaging of the pill is acceptable and not that the pill itself is appropriate and effective. The failure to extend the analysis beyond the 'packaging' encourages the persistence of discriminatory practices which allow stereotypes to perpetuate (1994:7).*

The inadequacies inherent in the multicultural approach to service provision to minority ethnic communities led to an alternative approach being advocated by academics and social care professionals interested in developing a framework which would be better suited to meeting the needs of these communities. This perspective was termed the 'anti-racism' approach. The anti-racism orientation acknowledges that the needs of the minority ethnic communities may be different, but maintains that these emerge from the experience of racism and may therefore require a significant change in practice (Butt and Mirza, 1996). This approach, therefore, directs attention towards the role played by institutions in perpetuating racism in society and the experiences of racism shared by all minority ethnic groups.

This perspective was instrumental in the adoption of the term 'black' to symbolise the political identity shared by all non-white minority groups which were subject to individual or institutional racism.

However, this approach is also not without its critics, such as Gilroy (1990) and Modood (1988). Ahmad et al. (1998) note that this political and intellectual stance attracted criticism from 'those on the right for its presumed excesses while at the same time being criticised from within for its rigidity, orthodoxy and refusal to accept that other aspects of personal or group identity (culture, religion) were legitimate bases for political organisation, defining needs or action' (p13). Patel et al. (1998) have also highlighted the role played by religion in the identity formation of different minority ethnic groups and the need for service providers to include this critical variable in their equation when planning and providing services. Furthermore, Macey (1995) points out that the anti-racism perspective denies people of dual heritage 'the right to choose their identities' and by insisting on the 'monolithic term black, comes close to denying their very existence' (p134). These views are summarised succinctly by Modood (1994a) thus:

> the error of the 1980s was to encourage colour-identities and discourage religious and other identities... A new public philosophy of racial equality and pluralism must aspire to bring into harmony the pluralism which exists on the ground, not to pit it against itself by insisting that some modes of collectivity trump all others (p32).

Current service provision to minority ethnic communities is still influenced to a large extent by the multi-cultural perspective and to a much lesser extent by the anti-racist perspective. The next section examines the role of race relations and other relevant legislation in UK in shaping service provision to minority ethnic communities.

RACE RELATIONS AND OTHER RELEVANT LEGISLATION

The Race Relations Act was first enacted in Britain in 1965 to counter racial discrimination, and in 1997 in Northern Ireland as the Race Relations (NI) order. The Race Relations Act was superseded by a revised Act in 1968 and finally the government of the day enacted a revised version in1976, which expanded the scope of indirect discrimination and gave the newly established Commission for Racial Equality (CRE), the duty of promoting this legislation. The 1976 Act acted as a spur to statutory and voluntary service providers in Britain to improve their practice in relation to minority ethnic communities by eliminating racial discrimination, thereby promoting equality of opportunity. The CRE undertook reviews of the 1976 Act to gather supportive evidence to lobby for changes in both the procedure and the evidence required by the law to prove discrimination, but the call to make meaningful changes to the law was not heeded by the legislators (Luthra, 1997). The revision to the Act in 1994 incorporated minor changes, but it was not until the report written by the Macpherson Committee on the outcomes of the Stephen Lawrence enquiry was published, which highlighted the need to protect individuals against institutional racism, that the momentum to achieve significant change in the scope of the Race Relations Act reached a critical point.

The last quarter of 2000 saw the Race Relations (Amendment) Act receive Royal Assent. Its main provisions came into force in the spring of 2001. This, the first major reform of the Race Relations Act, strengthens and extends the scope of the 1976 Act in two main ways: by extending the ambit of protection against racial discrimination by public authorities, and by placing a new, enforceable duty on public authorities (including voluntary agencies providing a service to members of the public) to tackle institutional racism, identified as a feature of institutional practice in the Macpherson report on the Stephen Lawrence enquiry.

In the late 1980s and the 1990s, for the first time in the history of social care provision in the UK, legislation was enacted which introduced a duty for social service departments and other agencies working to promote the welfare of children to 'give due consideration' to children's 'religious persuasion, racial origin and cultural and linguistic background' when making decisions about them. The Children Act 1989, for England and Wales, the Children (NI) Order 1995 and the Children (Scotland) Act 1995 provided the 'push' the social care sector needed to address sensitively and adequately the needs of minority ethnic children. It remains to be seen whether this has been sufficient to meet the requirements of the 2000 Race Relations (Amendment) Act. The next section examines research evidence to ascertain what impact, if any, the race relations and other legislation has had on social care provision for minority ethnic communities.

WHAT DOES RESEARCH TELL US

Research undertaken to examine the level and quality of service provision to minority ethnic communities has unequivocally revealed the gaps between the needs of the service users, and the level and quality of service provided whether the service provider is from the voluntary or the statutory sector.

A review of provision of services to Black families by the NSPCC's child protection teams, carried out by Jones and Butt (1995) led them to conclude that a great deal of confusion and inactivity surrounded work with Black families, and interestingly, although 50 out of 61 teams surveyed were working with Black children and families, the organisation was seen as a white organisation providing services for mainly white clients. It was argued by the researchers that although there was evidence of specialist Black projects being established, and of recruitment of Black workers, there was little indication of how the mainstream social care services were to be altered to meet the needs of Black children and families.

These findings are echoed in the research undertaken by Barn, Sinclair and Ferdinand (1997) in three social service departments. The purpose of their study was to examine how the departments were meeting the needs of minority ethnic families and children. One of their findings was that local authorities needed to develop adequate management information systems centring on race and ethnicity, including information on religion, language and diet, in order to address and meet the needs of minority ethnic children appropriately to promote their welfare and ensure their protection.

Further evidence that race relations legislation and the Children Act have not yet had sufficient impact on service provision to minority ethnic families emerged from a recent inspection of eight social services departments (SSDs) by the Social Services Inspectorate (O'Neale, 2000). The inspection revealed that most SSDs did not have adequate strategies in place to deliver appropriate services to minority ethnic families, and that children and families were often offered services that did not meet their needs appropriately or sensitively.

Research has also clearly demonstrated that services provided by the statutory sector, although much needed by minority ethnic families, often remain inaccessible to them. A survey of 84 family centres, in nine local authority areas, by Butt and Box (1998), to examine their use by Black families, led them to conclude that although the families using the centres found them to be critical in ensuring their survival, the majority of the centres did not appear to be accessible to Black families in need. This study goes beyond the limited user satisfaction surveys which reveal little about the appropriateness and adequacy of services, since the majority of the vulnerable service users are grateful to receive what little they are given and are loath to criticise services. The study also found that the adoption of equal opportunities policies (EOPs) by the family centres did not guarantee the accessibility of services for Black families. Connelly (1989) has argued that not all statutory service providers associated adoption of EOPs with altered outcomes for minority ethnic communities in their catchment area.

Another study which has explored the use of family support services by South Asian families was undertaken by Qureshi, Berridge and Wenman (2000), in one social services department. They also found that a major barrier to parents accessing family support was lack of information about available services, although comments from Asian parents revealed similar needs for family support and professional help as indigenous families. Other factors revealed by the study which led to a low level of family support for Asian families and a low level of access by these families included: the lack of specific policies focusing on social service provision to South Asian families; very few professionals and no senior managers from the South Asian community in the department; negative assumptions about South Asian families; and lack of confidence and skills in the departmental staff to develop culturally appropriate services.

Some of the gaps in service provision by the statutory and the voluntary sector, such as lack of accessible and appropriate services, have had to be met by the burgeoning Black voluntary sector. The crucial role played by the Black voluntary sector in meeting the needs of Black communities was revealed in a survey carried out by Butt and Box in 1997. The skills of this sector in providing appropriate services in an acceptable way within an environment of trust and underpinned by values shared by their users, were recognised by respondents from a range of agencies in the private and public sectors. However, the researchers cautioned against assuming that service provision by the Black voluntary sector was comprehensive, as some necessary services were not provided by these organisations. Additionally, they pointed out that these agencies are not in a position to make up for the limitations of social care provision by the statutory sector.

If the needs of minority ethnic communities are to be met in a comprehensive and appropriate manner, then all sectors within the community must co-ordinate their efforts in a more strategic manner as Dutt (1998) has argued. While acknowledging the valuable role played by specific services developed by both statutory and voluntary organisations, she contends that organisations need to develop a strategy to meet the social care needs of Black communities in the short term and the long term before selecting the approach which would help them achieve their strategy objective. She suggests a range of options which the service providers could consider, including the development of specific in-house services; a combination of mainstream services modified to suit the needs of Black communities and specific in-house services; and the development of the mainstream services combined with resourcing the Black voluntary sector to provide social care. The only criteria which should influence the choice of any of these options should be what best serves the interests of the service users.

This brief review of recent research highlights the extent to which the social care needs of children and families from minority ethnic communities remain unmet within an appropriate cultural framework.

OVERVIEW OF THE BOOK

This collection is not intended to be a catalogue of Barnardo's work with minority ethnic communities, but is a selection of models of practice which have been developed in the context of our work with the most disadvantaged and marginalised sections within the minority ethnic communities, such as young carers, those excluded from schools, disabled children and children without families.

The first paper in this collection, by Lenehan, Morrison and de Berker, is concerned with the model developed by three Barnardo's projects in the East London area to support minority ethnic families with disabled children. In the next contribution, by Newman, the emphasis shifts from appropriate models of care provided to disabled children, to caregiving by young people from minority ethnic communities to their parents or siblings. This chapter identifies some of the issues faced by this group of young people and outlines the work underway in some of the Barnardo's projects to offer a culturally appropriate service to minority ethnic young carers.

Chapter 4, by Curtis, takes as its subject the exclusion of African Caribbean young people and puts forward a model developed in consultation with the local Black community in Bristol to address this issue. The fifth chapter, by Coombe and Maan, focuses on the support provided to the Muslim community in Yorkshire by a project whose staff used the principles of systems theory to develop their practice in consultation with the community.

The final contribution in this collection provides a Scottish perspective on the adoption and fostering of children from the South Asian community. The authors describe an initiative which emerged out of the need to find suitable family placements for an increasing number of children from minority ethnic families, referred by social services to the Barnardo's Scotland family placement project. The 'Khandan' (meaning family) Initiative, the only one of its kind in Scotland, has engendered a great deal of interest from minority ethnic families interested in adopting, fostering or providing respite care to minority ethnic children. The South Asian worker appointed through funding provided by the Scottish Executive, noted in an article for Community Care, that 'the needs of black children can be met *when* [author's emphasis] a relevant strategy is in place' (Singh, 1999:5).

The conclusion picks up the strands emerging from the five very different models of practice with different minority ethnic communities described in this collection, with the objective of eliciting what appear to be the common ingredients of sensitive and appropriate practice with minority ethnic communities.

A WAY FORWARD

These models of practice have been planned and developed over a number of years by staff – both white and minority ethnic – in consultation with users from the minority ethnic communities whose needs they are intended to meet. The models need to be constantly reviewed so that they can be modified and refined, as more is learnt and understood about the needs of minority ethnic service users, and as the range of these needs changes in the new decade and beyond.

It is imperative that any innovative practice is subject to evaluation so that its effectiveness can be ascertained. It is not enough to have good intentions. Any and all practice must be shown to deliver outcomes which are needed and desired by those whose lives are impacted on by that practice. It is doubly crucial if that practice is directed at vulnerable children, young people and communities. Barnardo's has a strong tradition of ensuring that its practice uses the most effective approach to delivering childcare. As the Working Party established in 1966 noted, 'we consider that research by a qualified research worker into the results of our child care, including our work for coloured children, is urgently required if the best possible methods are to be evolved for the future' (Barnardos, Working Party on Racial Integration, 1966: 37).

REFERENCES

Ahmad W.I.U and Atkin K. (eds) (1996) *'Race' and Community Care*, Open University Press, Buckingham.

Ahmad W., Darr A., Jones L. and Nisar G. (1998) *Deafness and Ethnicity: Services, Policy and Politics*, The Policy Press, Bristol.

Atkin K. and Rollings J. (1993) *Community Care in a Multi-Racial Britain: A Critical Review of the Literature*, HMSO, London.

Barn R. (1993) *Black Children in the Public System*, B T Batsford, London, in association with British Agencies for Adoption and Fostering.

Barn R., Sinclair R. and Ferdinand D. (1997) Acting on Principle: *An Examination of Race and Ethnicity in Social Services Provision for Children and Families*, British Agencies for Adoption and Fostering, London.

Barnardo T.J. (1890) *Something Attempted Something Done*, William Clowes and Sons Limited, London.

Barnardos, Working Party on Racial Integration (1966), *Racial Integration and Barnardo's: Report of a Working Party*.

Brown B. (1994) 'Thinking it over: the terminology of "race". *Multicultural Teaching*, 12(2) Spring, pp22-23.

Butt J. and Box L. (1997) *Supportive Services, Effective Strategies*, Race Equality Unit.

Butt J. and Box L. (1998) *Family Centred: The Use of Family Centres by Black Communities*, Race Equality Unit.

Butt J., Gorbach P. and Ahmad B. (1994) *Equally Fair? A Report on Social Service Departments' Development, Implementation and Monitoring of Services for Black and Minority Ethnic Communities*, HMSO, London.

Butt J. and Mirza K. (1996) *Social Care and Black Communities: A Review of Recent Research Studies*, HMSO, London.

Caesar G., Parchment M. and Berridge D. (1993) *Research into Services for Black Children and Young People and Their Families in Barnardo's Midlands Division*, National Children's Bureau, London.

Connelly N. (1989) *Race and Change in Social Services Departments,* Policy Studies Institute.

Dominelli L. (1997) *Anti Racist Social Work* Second edition, British Association of Social Work.

Dutt R. (1998) 'The best for black users' *Community Care*, 30 April – 6 May.

Gilroy P. (1990) 'The end of anti-racism', in Ball W. and Solomons, J (eds) *'Race' and Local Politics*, Macmillan, Basingstoke.

Jones A. and Butt J. (1995) *Taking the Initiative*, National Society for the Prevention of Cruelty to Children, London.

Luthra M. (1997) *Britain's Black Population: Social Change, Public Policy and Agenda*, Arena, Aldershot.

Macey M. (1995) 'Towards racial justice? A re-evaluation of anti-racism' *Critical Social Policy*, **44/45**, pp126-146.

Mann-Kler D. (1997) *Out of the Shadows: An Action Research Report into Families, Racism and Exclusion in Northern Ireland*, Barnardo's Tuar Ceatha Project, Belfast.

Modood T. (1988) 'Who's defining Who?' *New Society*, 4 March, pp4-5.

Modood T. (1994a) 'Ethnicity and complexity', in *Challenge, Change and Opportunity: Overview, Texts and Agenda. The Future of Multi-ethnic Britain: Report on the Conference, University of Reading*, Autumn, The Runnymede Trust, London.

Modood T. (1994b) 'Political blackness and British Asians', *Sociology*, **28**(4), pp859-876.

Modood, T. (1996) 'The changing context of 'race' in Britain: a symposium', *Patterns of Prejudice* **30**(1), pp3-13.

O'Neale, V. (2000) *Excellence Not Excuses: Inspection of Services for Ethnic Minority Children and Families*, Department of Health, London.

Patel N., Naik D. and Humphries B. (1998) *Visions of Reality: Religion and Ethnicity in Social Work*, Central Council for Education and Training in Social Work, London.

Qureshi T., Berridge D. and Wenman H. (2000) *Where to Turn? Family Support for South Asian Communities,* National Children's Bureau, London.

Shah R. and Hatton C. (1999) *Caring Alone: Young Carers in South Asian Communities*, Barnardo's, Barkingside.

Singh S. (1999) 'Developing same-race placements'. *Community Care: Inside Supplement.* 28 January – 3 February.

Singh S. and Patel V. K. P. (1998) *Regarding Scotland's Black Children: Policy, Practice and Provision*, Barnardo's Family Placement Services and Scottish Black Workers Forum, Glasgow.

Yinger J.M. (1976) 'Ethnicity in complex societies', in Coser, L. and Larsen O.(eds) *The Uses of Controversy in Sociology*, Free Press, New York.

2 Disability, diversity and community services:

the East London experience

Christine Lenehan, Jan Morrison and Andrea de Berker

INTRODUCTION

This chapter looks at the development of services to disabled children in the multi racial, multi cultural East London boroughs of Newham, Tower Hamlets and Waltham Forest. This is followed by a description of how three Barnardo's projects in these localities have developed needs-led services for the range of communities within their boroughs.

SERVICE FOR DISABLED CHILDREN – THE BACKGROUND

Community service provision for disabled children began to develop in the 1970s. Early provision was poor and patchy and took little note of children's needs, being a service that concentrated solely on relieving parental stress. Maureen Oswin, in her introduction to the revised edition of *They Keep Going Away* comments it would not be an exaggeration to say that short term care throughout the 1970s, and at the start of the 1980s was mostly a hotch-potch of ill defined plans being badly carried out. She goes on to say that the majority of short-term care services were merely a 'crude separation service' and in some cases resembled little more than the 'kennelling of children' (Oswin, 1991).

This miserable base line for all disabled children also led to the specific needs of Black and minority ethnic children being largely ignored. Moreover, despite handbooks such as *"Double Discrimination"* being issued in 1990 to highlight the specific needs and rights of communities, areas of good practice have been hard to find.

This chapter concentrates on the provision of family-based short break care, in-homecare and leisure services. These services, which emerged in significant number in the mid-1980s were set up to provide alternatives to residential and institutional care (Oswin, 1991).

This approach which, in essence, is based on creating an individual service for each child, thus mirroring the lives of non-disabled children, should result in services that reflect the needs of disabled children from all communities. However, this has not been the case. In 1991, Stalker and Robinson looked at the waiting lists of family-based short break services and found three distinct groups. They were children with challenging behaviour, children with complex care needs and children from Black and minority ethnic communities regardless of the complexity or otherwise of their disability.

In 1993, Robinson and Stalker also found that Black and Asian families remained under-represented as users of family-based schemes and over-represented amongst users of residential establishments and health care units. This is not because it is not possible to achieve success in working in partnership with communities, as we will go on to demonstrate, but because of the over-reliance on myths, values and attitudes in relation to Black and minority ethnic communities, that continues to pervade social welfare institutions.

Robina Shah comments in her 1995 book *The Silent Minority* that:

> *disability, of whatever kind, does not discriminate. It transcends all races, beliefs and cultures. It creates similarly profound emotional, practical and psychological experiences for all parents, wherever they are. Unfortunately, where families from minority ethnic groups are concerned, common sense about valid generalisation of attitudes towards disability is lost in the mists of ignorance and perceived cultural differences.*

WHAT THE LAW REQUIRES

Family-based short break services have their legal starting point in the 1977 Health and Public Services Act. Early services were built on a loophole within the Act which allowed disabled children to have respite care in places other than a hospital bed. While this provision in the legislation led to the growth of community-based schemes, originally in Leeds and Somerset, it did not provide a suitable framework or any safeguards. As a consequence, by the mid-1980s, the nearly 200 schemes which had developed from it varied immensely in the type and quality of service they provided.

This left many children in vulnerable and inappropriate placements which were rarely properly registered, monitored or reviewed. This lack of clarity also meant that local authorities were unable to focus appropriately and adequately on the specific needs of this group of children and their families.

2

The 1989 Children Act was a positive step forward as it was instrumental in the identification of disabled children as 'children in need' and in bringing family-based short-term breaks into the same legal framework as other children accommodated by a local authority.

The 1980s had also seen a growing awareness of the importance of a child's racial, cultural, religious and linguistic inheritance, and the Children Act reinforced the need for this awareness, with the inclusion of a requirement that these factors should be taken into account within service provision.

The Children Act also importantly laid out the clear principle that the welfare of the child was the 'paramount consideration' when the state intervened in a child's life. The history of services for disabled children had often meant that children's needs were not recognised, let alone considered as being of paramount importance. The Children Act laid a duty on social welfare services to meet this requirement for the first time.

SERVICE PROVISION IN THE UK

The provision of short break schemes for disabled children throughout the country is variable not only in terms of size of schemes but also the level and diversity of the services offered and the children they cater for. The Children in Need Census undertaken in February 2000 identified 11,500 children currently receiving overnight short break placements. Most schemes are provided through local authorities, with a significant minority provided by voluntary agencies – Barnardo's is currently the largest voluntary sector provider.

A stark picture emerges, however, when service provision to minority ethnic communities is examined. Research studies over the last decade (Baxter, 1990; Robinson and Stalker, 1998; Chamba et al. 1999) echo a consistent message about the clear under-representation of Black and ethnic minority children within short break schemes. In *Ethnicity, Disability and Chronic Illness* (Ahmad, 2000), the author concluded that '...disability is at least as prevalent in black and minority ethnic communities as in other sectors of the population and should therefore receive equivalent levels of service'. Hence, the goal for all schemes must be that the children on the scheme roughly represent the demographic picture within the local community. Few local authorities or voluntary agencies have managed this. There are, however, some notable exceptions, including Bradford, and the provision developed by Barnardo's, to which we now turn.

THE LOCAL CONTEXT

Within Barnardo's East London projects, demographic and placement information is as follows:

Table 1: Percentages of service users compared to the total population of children in the East London Boroughs of Tower Hamlets, Newham and Waltham Forest

Borough	Tower Hamlets		Newham		Waltham Forest	
Ethnicity	Total child population	Project users	Total child population	Project users	Total child population	Project users
White	32.1%	31.5%	36.5%	15.3%	57%	27%
Black Caribbean	4.2%	2.5%	7.3%	14.1%	5%	8%
Black African	4.9%	9.6%	10.6%	28.2%	5%	5%
Indian	0.9%	0.3%	15.9%	7.7%	4.5%	20%
Pakistani	0.8%	0.3%	10.3%	21.8%	13%	32%
Bangladeshi	51.4%	54.5%	9.3%	8.9%	1%	0%
Chinese	1.1%	0%	0.7%	2.5%	5.5%	0%
Other	3.4%	1.3%	3.1%	1.3%	–	8%

It is clear from the table that disabled children from ethnic minorities are well represented as users of the three projects.

PROJECT DEVELOPMENT

The three Barnardo's projects work in partnership with their respective local authority social services departments (SSDs): Families Together with Tower Hamlets, Hamara Family Project with Waltham Forest and Family Link with Newham. Families Together was established first in 1987, Hamara followed in 1990 and Family Link came on line in 1994. In many ways, the success of Families Together paved the way for the other two projects and gave Barnardo's the confidence to continue to commit resources to this area of work.

The three East London boroughs are similar in that they are all culturally very diverse, although the proportion of different minority groups (all age groups) in each borough is very different:

- Tower Hamlets has a population of 176,000 and is 59% white, 31% Asian (mostly from the Sylhet region of Bangladesh), 3.5% Black Caribbean, 3% Black African and 5% from other minority communities (1991 Census)

- Newham has a population of 228,800 and is 50% white, 30% Asian (this is a very mixed group from many communities and faiths from the sub continent), 8% Black Caribbean, 9% Black African and 3% from other minority communities (1991 Census)

- Waltham Forest has a population of 220,200 and is 67.5% white, 15.5% Asian (mostly from Pakistan), 7.5% Black Caribbean, 4.5% Black African and 5% from other minority communities (1991 Census).

All three projects were initially contracted by the respective local authority SSDs to provide family-based short-break care whereby families are recruited as foster carers within the Children Act Regulations and offer short stays in their homes to disabled children. These relationships are long-term, and all the projects have links still in existence from the projects' early days. They are all committed to a policy of same race care and have developed this further to include the language and religious needs of the children they place. This policy has had very clear benefits both in relation to the recruitment of carers and in establishing credibility with the parents of children, quite apart from the value the children have received from being placed in families which reflect and build on their own racial and cultural identity. All three projects have actively recruited staff teams that reflect the cultural diversity of the communities they serve.

The importance of this is recognised by Jenny Morris in her book *'Still Missing'?* (1998); she identifies successful services by the concerted effort exerted to provide placements for children where their race, language and religion are matched. She notes that these services have recognised the diversity of languages and cultures that are included within the general term 'Asian' and have thus avoided the inadequate and unacceptable generalisations criticised by others.

All three projects quickly recruited carers who could meet the needs of most of the children they were asked to place. Children who have proved harder to place include children with challenging behaviour and older children, particularly older children with restricted mobility, as almost none of the carers recruited have had adapted accommodation.

Gradually, however, all three projects have developed other services, which have increased the range of choice open to parents and children. These developments have varied according to the different local situations:

- Families Together has developed specialist weekend services for autistic children

- Hamara has provided integrated holiday schemes

- Family Link has developed age-appropriate Saturday groups and an overnight sitting service.

All three projects have developed sitting services offering both in-home and outreach care to those children with the most complex needs. All of these services have been developed with children's identity at the centre. Parent support groups on all the projects also reflect the make-up of the communities, and operate on both individual language and multi-language bases. Developing a project identity has also proved important in developing the confidence of parents and service providers. It has also helped in combating the stigma which can go along with accessing services. Training and social programmes help to carry on the momentum.

TAKE-UP OF SERVICES – WHAT HAS WORKED

The final part of this chapter considers the factors which contributed to the take-up of services by all communities.

The most significant factor has been the projects' commitment to a same race placement policy. The adoption and implementation of this policy sends a clear message that a child's racial identity is recognised as being of overruling importance, essential for children who suffer the double discrimination of race and disability. It also makes it explicit that the projects recognise that there are good child care providers in all communities and that whilst racism exists within our society, each community can best care for its own children.

In order to put this policy into practice, it has been crucial to recruit, train and retain carers, sitters and volunteers who reflect the communities served by each project.

Key actions have included:

- recruiting a staff team who reflect the community, bringing a knowledge of culture and traditions, language and positive statements about the communities

- developing a project ethos where, although specialist information is held by individuals, the whole project has a responsibility and commitment to working with all communities

- writing anti-discriminatory statements and policies in the project, of which *everyone* in the project is aware and within which they have agreed to work. These need regular monitoring and evaluation. In addition, there is a strong commitment to take appropriate action when they are not adhered to

- being creative in communicating and networking with community groups. For example, parents are asked if there is somebody from the community that they wish to nominate as a carer for their child. The community press is also used to recruit carers

- maintaining the same standards and assessing the same issues with applicants from all communities, while recognising that there will be different cultural expectations, values and life experiences which are equally valid

- communicating as a project through many languages. Translation of material provided a starting point, but the recruitment of staff with appropriate skills marked the next key step. This is backed again by the provision of appropriate interpreting facilities. The onus must remain on the project to provide relevant interpreting facilities, rather than the service user having to request this

- tracking demographics and referrals and asking why a community is not referring and how to make services accessible rather than assuming that this community does not need the service

- constantly acknowledging the project cannot always know the right way to do things but that they do want to learn, and accepting that there is always more which they can learn

- continually checking with community groups that the service being delivered is the one that meets their needs

- integrating racial and cultural diversity into the day-to-day life of the project, through food, festivals etc.

CONSTRAINTS AND OPPORTUNITIES

In the communities served by the projects, Black and Asian families are often experiencing multiple deprivation. The issues of racism and poverty dominate all the work and provide the greatest challenge. It is the issue of personal racism for white managers and the white institutions within which it operates which provides the first constraint. White managers need to spend time in all sorts of settings looking at the decisions made and checking that they do not adversely affect Black communities or ignore their needs. This has to be an ongoing process.

Multi racial services can only work in settings where everyone has been involved in learning about why racism is harmful to all children. This has been particularly important in Tower Hamlets, where racial violence and intolerance remain a significant issue. The issues around tackling white carers about racism and leading them to understand its real effects on children's growth and identity has been, and remains challenging, but continues to be seen as essential to the projects' future as a whole.

The projects continue to have a role as advocates within white institutions and to raise questions such as: Why does the case constantly have to be made for good translation and interpreting facilities? What is it that stops the dual language skills of staff being formally recognised?

The process of working with community groups is necessarily slow if real commitment and engagement is to be achieved. This contrasts sharply with an increasing market place approach to social welfare and a need to measure services against numbers and cost.

It has been necessary for the projects to take on a wider community development perspective than would usually be expected of a direct service provider. This has required, for example, that carers are trained in ways which act as a stepping stone to other opportunities; being involved in planning for services to meet a range of needs; and constant innovation and evaluation in partnership with families and communities.

Finally, there is a joy in celebrating racial and cultural diversity. It has enhanced the work of the projects, ensuring a better quality of care for all the children and families in receipt of services, demonstrating that service provision in a multicultural setting is possible, effective and rewarding.

REFERENCES

Ahmad W.I.U (ed.) (2000) *Ethnicity, Disability, and Chronic Illness*, Open University Press, Buckingham.

Baxter C. (1990) *Double Discrimination: Issues and Services for People with Learning Difficulties from Black and Ethnic Minority Communities*, Kings Fund, London.

Chamba R., Ahmad W., Hirst M., Lawton D. and Beresford B. (1999) *On the Edge: Minority Ethnic Families Caring for a Severely Disabled Child.*, The Policy Press, London.

Department of Health (2000) *Children in Need in England: First Results of a Survey of Activity and Expenditure as Reported by Local Authority Social Services' Children and Families Teams*, http://www.doh.gov.uk/public/cinresults.pdf

2

Great Britain (1977) The Health and Public Services Act, HMSO, London.

Great Britain (1989) The Children Act. HMSO, London.

Greater London Association of Disabled People (1996) *Ethnicity and Disability: Moving Towards Equity in Service Provision*, CVS Consultants, London.

Morris J. (1998) *Still Missing? Vol. 2: Disabled Children and the Children Act*, Who Cares? Trust, London.

Oswin M. (1991) *They Keep Going Away: A Critical Study of Short-term Residential Care Services for Children with Learning Disabilities*, King Edwards Hospital Fund for London, London.

Robinson C. and Stalker K. (1993) 'Patterns of provision in respite care and the Children Act', *British Journal of Social Work*, **21**(1) pp45-63.

Robinson C. and Stalker K. (1998) *Growing up with Disability*, Jessica Kingsley, London.

Shah R. (1995). *The Silent Minority: Children with Disabilities in Asian Families*, National Children's Bureau, London.

Stalker K. and Robinson C. (1991) *'You're on the Waiting List': Families Waiting for Respite Care Services*, Norah Fry Research Centre, Bristol.

Culture, ethnicity and caregiving:

3

the situation of Black and Asian young carers

Tony Newman

INTRODUCTION

Little over a decade ago, concern for children who undertake excessive caring roles within their households was primarily confined to therapeutic contexts, especially those working within the psychotherapeutic tradition that dealt with 'parentified' children (Boszormenyi-Nagy, 1965; Minuchin, 1974). Some children, it is suggested (Jurkovic, 1997) are endowed with premature adult roles because of parental pathology, typically originating in early emotional deprivation which results in parents tending to treat their own children as parental figures. However, outside the context of severely dysfunctional families, children's carrying out atypical caring duties in the household where the primary carer was ill or disabled was not until recently perceived as problematic. The substantial growth in consciousness that has taken place over this period, stimulated partly by the considerable demographic changes that have taken place in family structures, and partly by the growing awareness of children's rights issues, has resulted in a wide-ranging revision of how we respond to families where children's roles are strongly affected by parental incapacity.

This chapter focuses on young carers in general and on Black and Asian young carers in particular. It begins by sketching the wider picture with regard to all care givers in the United Kingdom and identifies the concerns and controversies this issue has generated. The findings from a Barnardo's survey bring into sharp relief the key issues facing all carers, including those from Black and Asian communities. The chapter then outlines the work undertaken by two Barnardo's projects in the Midlands and Yorkshire to develop a needs-led service, in response to the issues identified by the survey and as a result of feedback from young Asian and Black carers; conclusions are then drawn about future service provision to these young people.

3

YOUNG CARERS – THE BACKGROUND

The situation of children who undertake what is perceived as an excessive volume of domestic care for family members has emerged as a major child welfare concern in a period of little over a decade. From a baseline of close to zero, children who have become known as 'young carers' have generated a substantial body of research literature over this period (O'Neill, 1988; Bilsborrow, 1992; Aldridge and Becker, 1993; Becker et al. 1998), and are specifically recognised in Parliamentary legislation through the 1996 Carers (Recognition and Services) Act.

While definitions of young carers vary, the following has been widely adopted by Barnardo's:

> A 'young carer' is a child or young person under the age of 18 whose life is in some way restricted because of the need to take responsibility for a person who is ill, has a disability, is elderly, is experiencing mental distress or is affected by substance misuse.

Hence, the issue of the restrictions on normal activities, rather than simply any tasks undertaken, is considered to be the most pertinent issue.

Barnardo's was one of the first child care organisations to recognise and respond to this issue, and now delivers services to young carers and their families from many locations throughout the United Kingdom. The circumstances of young carers have been the subject of publicity campaigns by several child care charities, including the Princess Royal Trust for Carers, NCH Action for Children, the Children's Society, the Women's Institute and Barnardo's. The situation of young carers has not just been a concern of social care services, as clinicians have also expressed concern for their emotional and physical health (Jenkins and Wing, 1994). The Government's National Strategy on Carers, published in 1999, contains a separate chapter on young people. In short, 'young carers' are well and truly on the map of child welfare services.

QUESTIONS AND DISPUTES

The rapid rise to prominence of this issue has generated a number of questions and a few controversies. Firstly, while widely accepted and used within the lexicon of child welfare terminology, the term 'young carer' is in many ways a professional convenience, not always recognised and accepted by children and young people themselves. Secondly, some disabled people have expressed concern, and even anger, that they may be seen as the source of their child's problem, instead of the problem being located in the level of support the family receives. The perceived focus on supporting children rather than supporting parents has been disputed as further pathologising disabled people (Keith and Morris, 1995), a criticism that has been at least partly recognised by those working within the field by an increased emphasis on whole family support (Becker et al. 1998). Currently, it is widely recognised that both children and their parents may need support, sometimes separately, sometimes together, and that an approach which considers the whole family is most likely to prove fruitful. Thirdly, a concern that the expansion of young carer services has run ahead of any robust research about their circumstances has been expressed (Olsen, 1996), though the value and validity of contemporary research has also been vigorously defended (Aldridge and Becker, 1996). Fourthly, there has been remarkably little exploration of the *effectiveness* of young carer services, with the large majority of published studies relying almost entirely on weak methodologies, such as selected personal accounts (for example, Crabtree and Warner, 1999; Frank et al. 1999) rather than those utilising control or comparison groups (for an exception, undertaken in a Barnardo's service, see Taggart, 1999). It has therefore been recognised that practice in services for young carers needs to build on previous work by developing a stronger evidence base for its effectiveness (Becker et al. 1998).

Finally, and most pertinently to our discussion, it remains unclear whether the assumptions made, structures created and interventions undertaken by young carer services are equally applicable to *all* children in the UK population. Young carer services are located within the complex and sensitive arena of reciprocal family obligations, expectations and duties. While the obligations of children to their parents feature powerfully in both Eastern and Western religious traditions, the ethical architecture of young carers work has emanated from secular sources, particularly human rights discourse, which is primarily concerned with the autonomy of the individual rather than the individual's perceived obligations to others. A list of rights that should be extended to young carers (Young Carers Research Group, 1994), which has been widely replicated in young carer service operational policies, illustrates this dilemma. The diminution of obligation, and the concomitant emphasis on the primacy of the child's welfare, might lead us to theorise that in circumstances where the child's obligations to her parents dominate, rather than the primacy of her needs a different kind of approach may be required of child welfare services.

ETHNICITY AND CHILDREN'S CAREGIVING

Large-scale surveys of children already known to young carer services, while suffering from a lack of representation, are able, given their much larger numbers, to investigate the relationship between variables much more comprehensively. What do we know of the prevalence of children's care giving among minority ethnic communities in the UK? In the absence of representative samples which have ethnicity as a variable, the answer is inevitably, 'not a lot'. While the issue has been highlighted from the broader perspective of needing to ensure the equitable distribution of child welfare services (Arthur and Wiffin, 1995), little detailed information is available. One attempt to carry out a survey of minority ethnic group children who are also young carers was largely unsuccessful. Of a thousand information packs distributed in three schools in Hammersmith and Fulham, 140 responses were received, with 26 children self-identifying as 'young carers' (Hendessi, 1996; Mapp, 1996). None, however, were boys, presenting obvious questions about representation. A Barnardo's survey, carried out in 1998, does give some insight into the issue, though it should be stressed that the sample consisted of children and young people known to Barnardo's young carer services, rather than a sample drawn from a general population.

THE 1998 BARNARDO'S SURVEY

Of the 299 children reported by the survey, 42% were male and 58% female. The average age was just over 12 years. Types of care provided are shown in Figure 1.

Figure 1 – Percentage of carers providing different types of care

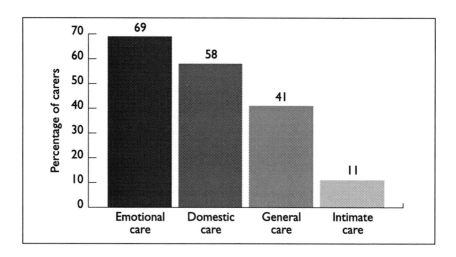

Many children were reported as providing more than one form of care, with 13% of children providing care for more than one person. Thirty-two per cent of the population of 'cared for' people were single parents with mental illnesses (including schizophrenia, depression and phobic conditions). Where the person cared for was the mother (single or not), the disabling condition was, in 60% of cases, a mental illness.

Staff completing the questionnaire were asked to describe the main condition of the care receiver that was precipitating the provision of care by the child. In almost three-quarters of cases, the primary recipient of care was the mother. In less than 20% of cases, it was a sibling, with fathers accounting for only 6% of care receivers.

Aggregating the conditions of care receivers into impairment clusters, as illustrated below in Figure 2, psychological disorders were found to predominate. In the learning disability (intellectual) category, the care-receivers are siblings of young carers, not adults. Aggregated psychological disorders includes drug/alcohol abuse.

Figure 2 – Parental and sibling impairments

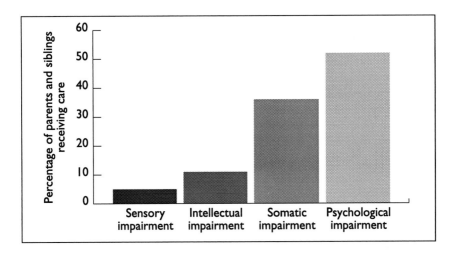

The referrals received by Barnardo's projects were mostly from statutory sources:

■ as one might expect, 63% of those referred by *education* were missing school (74% of whom were female). Almost 90% were aged 13 and over. Only one child aged under 13 referred by education was missing school. Parental mental illness accounted for 63% of all education referrals, and 15% of children were reported as being involved in intimate care

■ social services departments accounted for the majority of referrals. Almost three-quarters of referrals were single parent families; 16% of children in these families were involved in intimate care and 19% were reported as missing school. Almost 60% of parents in the families had mental disorders

■ over half (56%) of those referred by *health* were 12 years and under; there were an equal number of one- and two-parent families. Seventeen per cent of children were missing school; a quarter of parents were depressed, whereas a further two thirds (61% in all) were mentally ill.

While the above patterns inevitably reflect the particular responsibilities and concerns of the referring agencies, the phenomenon of parental psychological illness remains a common theme. Where the parent was physically disabled, 14% of referrals came from relatives. The largest number of 'relative' referrals was from families with a learning disabled child (38%). Where referrals were from children *themselves*, in over half the cases (51%), the parent had a somatic disorder, indicating that children may find it easier to request help when a parent has a physical disability than a psychological disorder.

The Barnardo's dataset indicates that in only 38% of cases is a second adult present in the home where the primary care receiver is affected by a psychological illness; in the case of a somatic illness, this rises to 66%. A family where the main carer is affected by a psychological illness may impact on a child in a very different way, and require a range of support skills quite different from that where the main carer has a physical impairment. If this dataset suggests a 'typical' family where a young carer might be located, it is in a family where a lone female parent is affected by a psychological illness.

Parental illness – impact on children

What impact do different types of parental illness have on young carers? The only hard data we have here is on school absences. If we isolate the care receiver condition of 'mental illness' the single largest category, accounting for a third of the total – the population consists of 71% lone parents, almost three-quarters of whom have more than one child. In 29% of lone-parent families, the child with caring duties is reported as missing school. As the mean percentage of children missing school is 19%, and the mean ages of this population and the total population are similar (12.7 and 12.1 years respectively), the context of children living in a lone-parent family where the adult is affected by a mental illness indicates a heightened level of potential vulnerability.

Conflating all care receiver conditions into psychological and somatic, we can see the highly significant impact of psychological illnesses.

Table 1 – Effect of parental impairment on school absences

	Psychological illnesses*	Somatic illnesses**
Missing school	43	14
Not missing school	109	128

* Includes mental illness, drug and alcohol addiction, phobic conditions, depression and ME.

** Includes learning disability, arthritis, physical disability, chronic illness, cancer, cerebral palsy, stroke, impaired mobility, spina bifida, multiple sclerosis, epilepsy, blindness, deafness and asthma.

As Table 1 shows, psychological illness is far more strongly associated with school absences overall than somatic disorders. Non-psychological disorders of any kind, according to this dataset, have less serious impacts on school attendance, though it must be noted that in the case of both alcohol and drug dependent parents, school absenteeism was high; however, numbers were too small for calculation. Three-quarters of all school absenteeism occurred in families where a psychological illness had been reported. The extent of the causal relationship between these two phenomena, without additional information on the socio-economic context of the families is, however, speculative – substantially higher levels of poverty in lone-parent households, for example, would be expected to reduce school attendance regardless of the psychological health of the parent.

While the drawbacks to this survey are numerous – insufficient confidence in representation, definitional problems and at least partially corrupted data – the emphasis that emerges from the data focuses on the relative primacy of parental psychological disorders, especially when associated with lone parenthood. Both in terms of prevalence, and the capacity of parental mental illness to potentiate poorer child outcomes when associated with economic deprivation and negative parental affect, this is congruent with what we know of how parental illness impacts on children. In this important dimension, the Barnardo's data differs from that in the 1997 national survey conducted by the Loughborough University Young Carers Research Group, which concluded that 'the majority of young carers are caring for people with physical health problems, the most commonly occurring single condition being MS' (Aldridge and Becker, 1998:13).

3

Black and Asian young carers

What did this survey tell us about young carers from Black and Asian communities? Their profile in this survey is illustrated below.

Table 2 – Ethnicity (categories provided to respondents)

White	87%
Black Caribbean	2%
Black African	1%
Black Other	2%
Indian	2%
Pakistani	3%
Bangladeshi	–
Chinese	<1%
Other Asian	2%

As we can see, children from Black and Asian communities comprised around 13% of children referred. Almost half (47%) of their parents were lone parents, compared to 61% from white families. Over half of all ethnic minority parents (56%) were affected by psychological illnesses, compared to 46% of white parents. While there were other minor differences in the profile of white children compared to minority ethnic children, these differences were small, and not statistically significant. As we can see, while some differences are evident, the sample is insufficiently large to give us confidence that these differences are associated with ethnicity. In common with other surveys of this size, we are also unable to differentiate between different minority ethnic groups, and hence run the risk of assuming a level of commonality which is illusory. In order to develop support services which are appropriate to the needs of children from different minority ethnic communities, we need more detailed information which can illuminate any important differences in their circumstances.

EXPECTATIONS AND OBLIGATIONS – DIFFERENCES BETWEEN WHITE AND MINORITY ETHNIC COMMUNITIES

We know from extensive survey evidence (Berthoud and Jowell 1997) that family structures – and the views of members – of British citizens from African-Caribbean and Asian communities may differ in some ways from white British families. While significant differences are typically found *between* South Asian communities, particularly between Bangladeshi, Pakistani and Indian families, differences have also been noted between all these groups as compared to white families. These include a stronger antipathy to divorce, less willingness for women to work outside the home, a preference for multi-generational households, a greater division of labour by gender, a more positive attitude towards marriage and a correspondingly negative attitude towards co-habitation prior to marriage (Beishon et al. 1998). An enhanced role for intra-family obligations has been noted in other communities in which religious belief and practice may play a proportionately greater role (for example, within Jewish families, see Freedman (1996)). While the importance of intra- and inter-family support in migrant communities has been emphasised (Ahmad, 1996), changes in cultural expectations have also been noted, as has the accumulation of greater cultural capital by children of migrants, and the corresponding effect this may have on normative values associated with family obligations (Modood et al, 1994). In addition, social class is known to be a powerful mediator of family obligations (Finch, 1989), a factor that has been noted as differentiating some dimensions of kinship support not just in white communities but also in working class compared to middle class South Asian communities (Werbner, 1990). The stereotypes of both the endlessly supportive extended migrant family and, conversely, the oppressive restraint on young British Asians of traditional cultures, unfortunately retain their power (Atkin and Rollings, 1996). Adding cultural expectations, particularly in the context of inter-generational change, to the already complex brew of gender and class is likely to challenge further our understanding of the way in which obligations are fulfilled within families.

Nonetheless, given the relatively low prevalence of young carers in the population (whatever method of calculation is used) and the variations that exist in all populations, it is unclear to what extent these apparent differences will retain their relevance when the experiences of children are examined. Furthermore, given the accumulation of inter-generational differences experienced by any migrant population, we cannot be sure whether the views and experiences of minority ethnic children and white children will differ as significantly as that of their parents. However, given the extensive evidence that patterns of family structure, cultural expectations and reciprocal obligations between parent and child differ in minority ethnic families compared to white families – either in form or in degree of intensity -we might expect to find a correspondingly different kind of 'young carer experience'.

How prominently do children and young people from Black and Asian communities feature in dedicated young carer services nationally? The Barnardo's data base is inevitably limited and hence we cannot estimate this with any certainty. While two specific Black and Asian young carer services are reported in the 1998 handbook of young carers projects (Aldridge and Becker, 1998), and four more services highlight their work with Black and Asian children, most make no mention of this dimension of work. However, one detailed examination of the situation of children in South Asian communities has recently been published by Barnardo's, and its conclusions can, until more information emerges, be regarded as the 'best evidence' we have to date.

BARNARDO'S WORK WITH YOUNG CARERS FROM MINORITY ETHNIC COMMUNITIES

An in-depth study of the experiences of 19 South Asian young people in contact with two Barnardo's young carer services in large English cities adds considerable detail to the sparse data discussed above (Shah and Hatton, 1999). All the quotes below are from young people who contributed to this study.

As in the Barnardo's survey, the majority of young people were caring for relatives – mostly mothers – with mental health problems. Many details in the study confirm or replicate similar explorations of young carers of any ethnic background. Children provided a wide range of support, emotional and physical, their lives were often highly restricted by their caring duties, and caring roles were not clearly differentiated by gender, with both boys and girls taking on considerable levels of responsibility. While young children were less likely to consider themselves 'carers', this identity became more central to the children's perception of themselves as they grew older. Few instances of support or assessment by statutory authorities were reported. For the older children, the consequences of caring, or even its indefinite continuation, were a constant factor. Interference with educational careers, especially reduced aspirations, was a frequent occurrence. Half of the young people reported racist bullying; several had come to accept this as a permanent part of their lives. The young people themselves felt their actual circumstances were little different from those of white carers; key differences, however, were reported as being in the expectations of both professionals and adults within their own families and community. Many professionals, the children reported, had expectations about the roles of young carers, based on perceptions of family obligation, gender and culturally specific roles. Shah and Hatton (1999) note that:

> ...it seemed to the young people in this study that the 'colour-blind' approach had sometimes been replaced by an approach which was regarded as 'culturally sensitive', but in fact relied on blanket stereotypes about different ethnic groups. (p61)

One young person commented:

> They seem very judgmental. They keep giving us an Asian social worker even though we've asked for non-Asian. They say mum's Asian, we say she can understand English (p61)

Young people also reported similar inappropriate expectations from relatives and other adults within their own communities, including unhelpful attitudes towards disability and mental illness.

> Instead of helping us the (South Asian) social worker would sit there and mock us. 'You're Asian, you can't do this you can't give up'. (p60)

> ...they think it's a curse, witchcraft, they think there's no clinical reason for it. I think that the people in my street they act a bit different to my mum, they know she's been in hospital so they think she will do something to me, or how is she going to act if I talk to her? (p54)

The study was instructive in highlighting both the similarities and the differences between the experiences of young people from different ethnic backgrounds. Young Asian carers reported having to deal with what they perceived as unreasonable and distorted expectations from those both within and outside their community. While the young people interviewed felt their experiences were little different from white children, where comparisons were made, they perceived a greater burden than their peers due to the greater difficulty of both asking for help, and the lesser likelihood of receiving it.

While differentiation between cultural, religious and ethnic groups is crucial where the needs and preferences of children and their families are correspondingly dissimilar, the lack of need for differentiation on many aspects of these children's lives must be noted also.

> I think most carers hate being patronised. Carers I've come across are still expected to hold adult responsibilities, but they're not told enough details, so I think people should remember to talk to them as adults, but remember that they are only still children, and do things in their best interest as children not adults. You get patronised then you get assessed as an adult, it's totally wrong. (Shah and Hatton, 1999: 63).

In several of Barnardo's young carer projects, such as those based in Leicester and Bradford, children from Black and Asian communities comprise around 30% of the total number of children referred, though in many other parts of the UK, numbers are inevitably much smaller. Rather than attempting to provide services to Black and Asian young carers in isolation, Barnardo's projects seek to work in collaboration with organisations that specifically serve particular minority ethnic groups. In Barnardo's Carefree Project in Leicester, a partnership has been developed with a local Asian mental health charity, with Barnardo's supplying the specialist knowledge on carers, and the local charity providing the detailed knowledge of their own community. Other collaborative relationships have been developed with organisations such as Crossroads and the Red Cross, which have developed targeted resources for Black and Asian adult carers; referrals and initial assessments are undertaken by the local Barnardo's young carer service and help is then delivered in association with these other charities. Other strategies have included public displays and information days, and liaison with religious and community leaders. However, the proportion of young people from Black and Asian communities helped by the service remains fewer than should be expected, given the respective proportions of children from these communities in the local population.

In Barnardo's young carers project in Bradford, feedback from users led to the appointment of a female project worker, as it was felt that this was likely to make the service more accessible and popular. Attention to practical details has helped also; activities in the Christmas period were shifted from daylight hours to the evening, to accommodate Muslim children during the period of Ramadan. An annual Eid party is organised and, recognising that attention must be given to numerically less represented groups, outreach work has been carried out in local Sikh temples. However, as with many other young carer services, recruitment of workers from minority ethnic groups has proved difficult, partly because of the continuing insecurity of short-term funding.

Both Barnardo's research and practice experience in this field have pointed towards similar conclusions. While sensitivity towards the needs of young people from different communities is essential, young carers from all backgrounds may perceive themselves as having more in common than the older generation of their parents and grandparents. Differentiation may be desirable in many cases – such as those illustrated above – but in many circumstances the needs of young people are very similar. Services will inevitably have to learn to balance the expectations of children and their parents, and will, in all probability, have to manage the dissonance between them.

CONCLUSION

Children, whether they are from minority ethnic groups or not, are most at risk where they are confronted by multiple adversities. This is highly relevant to what we know of young carers. The act of caring may be less important than the context in which it takes place. In seeking to help young carers and their families, young carer services have increasingly emphasised the *impact* on the child's health and development of the tasks they undertake, not just the nature of the tasks themselves. Some children undertaking quite demanding caring tasks, but who are not exposed to any additional risk factors, may be relatively unaffected. For other children, the presence of large numbers of risk factors may mean that even relatively minor exposure to caring tasks may result in damaging consequences.

The conflicting pressures that carers encounter are well known; the sense of obligation, the feeling of having no choice, the mixture of loyalty and resentment and, of course, the genuine desire to help a loved one. Many adult carers find these pressures difficult to bear. Children, who expect to receive, not deliver care, and are less emotionally equipped to deal with these pressures, may be under even more stress. However, the dividing line between excessive and normative 'caring' is a fine one and it is important both to identify those children suffering extreme hardships, and to avoid including children unjustifiably. The additional obstacles which young carers from minority ethnic communities face requires a response that neither seeks to suppress the common problems that all young people may face, nor ignore such differences when they emerge.

3

REFERENCES

Ahmad W.I.U. (1996) 'Family obligations and social change among Asian communities', in Ahmad W.I.U. and Atkin K. (eds) *'Race' and Community Care*, Open University Press, Buckingham.

Aldridge J. and Becker S. (1993) *Children Who Care: Inside the World of Young Carers.*: Young Carers Research Group, Loughborough University, Loughborough.

Aldridge J. and Becker S. (1996) 'Disability rights and the denial of young carers: the dangers of zero-sum arguments', *Critical Social Policy*, 16(3), pp. 55-76.

Aldridge J. and Becker S. (1998) *The National Handbook of Young Carers Projects 1998*. YCRG/Carers National Association, London.

Arthur V. and Wiffin J. (1995) 'A plea to practitioners'. *Community Care*, 26 October – 1 November, p.21

Atkin K, and Rollings J. (1996) 'Looking after their own? Family care giving among Asian and Afro-Caribbean communities', In Ahmad W.I.U. and Atkin K. (eds) *'Race' and Community Care*, Open University Press, Buckingham.

Becker S, Aldridge J. and Dearden C. (1998) *Young Carers and Their Families*, Blackwell Science, Oxford.

Beishon S, Modood T. and Virdee S. (1998) *Ethnic Minority Families*, Policy Studies Institute, Grantham.

Berthoud B.R. and Jowell R.M. (1997) *Fourth National Survey of Ethnic Minorities*, ESRC, London.

Bilsborrow S. (1992) 'You Grow Up Fast as Well...' Young Carers on Merseyside, Barnardo's, Barkingside.

Boszormenyi-Nagy I. (1965) 'A theory of relationships: experience and transaction', in Boszormenyi-Nagy I. and Framo J.L. (eds) *Intensive Family Therapy: Theoretical and Practical Aspects*, Harper and Row, New York

Crabtree H. and Warner L. (1999) *Too Much To Take On: A Report on Young Carers and Bullying*: Princess Royal Trust for Carers, London.

Department of Health (1999) *Caring about Carers: A National Strategy for Carers*, Department of Health, London.

Finch J. (1989) *Family Obligations and Social Change*. Polity Press, Cambridge.

Frank J., Tatum C. and Tucker S. (1999) On Small Shoulders: Learning From the Experiences of Former Young Carers. The Children's Society, London.

Freedman B. (1996) 'Respectful service and reverent obedience: a Jewish view on making decisions for incompetent parents', *Hastings Cent Rep.*, **26**, pp31-37

Hendessi M. (1996) *Report of the Survey of Young Carers in Hammersmith and Fulham*. Hammersmith and Fulham Social Services.

Hunt A; Fox J. and Morgan M. (1973) *Families and Their Needs with Particular Reference to One Parent Families: vol. II*, London.

Jenkins S. and Wing C. (1994) 'Who cares for young carers?' *British Medical Journal*, **308**, pp733-734.

Jurkovic G.J. (1997) *Lost Childhoods: The Plight of the Parentified Child,*. Brunner-Mazel, New York.

Keith L. and Morris J. (1995) 'Easy targets: a disability rights perspective on the "children as carers" debate', *Critical Social Policy*, **44/45**, pp36-57.

Mapp S. (1996) 'Shared learning'. *Community Care* 26 September – 2 October, p13.

Minuchin S. (1974) Cambridge, MA. *Families and Family Therapy*, Harvard University Press, Cambridge, MA.

Modood T, Beishon S. and Virdee S. (1994) *Changing Ethnic Identities*: Policy Studies Institute, London.

Newman T. (2000) Workers and helpers: perspectives on children's labour, 1899-1999, *British Journal of Social Work*, **30**(3), pp323-338.

O'Neill A. (1988) *Young Carers: the Thameside Research*, Tameside Metropolitan Borough Council.

Olsen R. (1996) 'Young carers: challenging the facts and politics of research into children and caring'. *Disability and Society*, 11(1), pp41-54.

Shah R. and Hatton C. (1999) Caring Alone: Young Carers in South Asian Communities. Barnardo's, Barkingside.

Taggart L. (1999) *An Examination of the Effectiveness of an Education Programme in Addressing the Psychological Needs of Young Carers in Northern Ireland*, University of Ulster, Department of Applied Psychology, unpublished BSc dissertation.

Werbner P. (1990) *The Migration Process: Capital, Gifts and Offerings Among British Pakistanis*, Berg, London.

Young Carers Research Group (1994) *Getting it Right for Young Carers : A Training Pack for Professionals*, Loughborough University/Crossroads, Loughborough.

3

Success in the face of adversity: 4

a partnership project to support minority ethnic pupils excluded from school

Katherine Curtis

INTRODUCTION

Education is one of the basic rights of all children, a right enshrined in the United Nations Convention on the Rights of the Child (1991) of which the United Kingdom is a signatory. Yet, thousands of children are excluded from both primary and secondary schools, with the exclusion rate for minority ethnic pupils being significantly greater than that of indigenous pupils. A number of research studies, including those carried out in South London, Birmingham, Wolverhampton, Sheffield and Nottingham, at the beginning of the 1990s, have all revealed a great over-representation of minority ethnic children within local populations of children excluded from school. Researchers and commentators have expressed specific concerns about young African-Caribbean children, identified by 1993/94 OFSTED inspection data to be six times more likely to be excluded than white pupils (Social Exclusion Unit, 1998).

This chapter examines the issue of exclusion of minority ethnic pupils from mainstream schools. The differential rates for exclusion of Black, Asian and indigenous pupils are highlighted before exploring some of the reasons behind these differences. Both short-term and long-term costs of excluding pupils from the education system are also commented on before taking a detailed look at the service response that has been developed in West England, in consultation with the Black community, to support and reintegrate African and Caribbean pupils excluded from mainstream schools.

EXCLUSION – THE STATISTICS

The 1990s saw a sharp rise in all permanent exclusions from maintained schools in England, to a peak of 12,461 in 1996/97. However this was followed by a fall in total exclusions of over 16% to 10,292 in 1998/89, accompanied by an even greater fall in the proportion of non-white exclusions (DfEE 2000). Indeed between 1996/97 and 1998/99 the percentage of black pupils (African Caribbean, Black African and Black Other) excluded from schools were reported to have fallen nearly twice as fast as exclusions of white pupils (DfEE 2000). Recent years have also seen levels of achievement amongst African-Caribbean pupils rise faster than among their white peers (DfEE, 2001).

Yet at the end of the 1990s, records still show black (African, African-Caribbean and Black Other) pupils to be greatly over-represented amongst the total population of children excluded from English schools. While only 0.15 per cent of white pupils were permanently excluded in 1998/99, 0.59 per cent of African Caribbean and 0.49 per cent of Black Other pupils were excluded. Black pupils were therefore nearly four times more likely to be excluded than white children (DfEE, 2000).

There is also evidence to suggest that concerns should move beyond the historical focus on young black – specifically African-Caribbean – boys. For example, staff surveyed across 30 local education authorities in England and Wales reported that rates of exclusion may be rising among Bangladeshi boys (Kinder et al., 2000). Likewise, an OFSTED study in 1996 reported an increasing number of LEAs to have concerns about the proportions of Pakistani boys being excluded from local schools.

Records have historically shown boys to be at far greater risk of exclusion than girls (DfEE 2000). However, over eight years ago studies showed that on a local level, African-Caribbean girls could be at as great a risk of exclusion as their male counterparts (Gillborn and Gipps, 1996); and LEA staff in Kinder et al.'s (2000) study reported that levels of exclusion among African-Caribbean girls may be rising.

GOING BEHIND THE STATISTICS ON EXCLUSION OF BLACK CHILDREN – WHY AND HOW

Gillborn and Gipps (1996) describe the particular effectiveness of qualitative research methods in digging out the 'why and the how' (p48) behind these statistics. Many qualitative studies have focused particularly on the relationship between teachers and their Black – mainly African or African Caribbean – pupils, drawing the following conclusions:

- These pupils were disciplined more often than their peers and were perceived by teachers as 'troublesome' (Driver, 1997; Wright, 1986; Gillborn and Drew, 1992; and Sewell, 1997)

- teachers' perceptions of these pupils caused them to react more readily to perceived challenges from this group as opposed to those from other pupils (Gillborn and Drew, 1992; Bourne, 1994; Cohen and Hughes, 1994; and Sewell, 1997)

- the way teachers responded to pupils' behaviour exacerbated the conflict which characterised their interactions with these pupils (Driver, 1997; Wright, 1986; Cohen and Hughes, 1994; and Sewell, 1997)

- pupils identified with and responded to teachers' expectations of low academic achievement and problematic behaviour (Wright, 1986; and Sewell, 1997)

- to achieve success in school, Black pupils must not only be talented and hard working, but also develop strategies to combat teachers' assumptions about them. This may involve them sacrificing the goodwill of their peer group (Sewell, 1997; Gillborn, 1990)

- pupils were sometimes responding to racist abuse from other pupils when breaking rules (Bourne, 1994; Cohen and Hughes, 1994).

Research has centred less on the relationships between young Asian pupils and their teachers. However, there is evidence that while young Black students are often regarded as 'truculent', Asian students are generally perceived as 'conformist'; and where they are the main ethnic group this can take on more negative connotations, for example students may be perceived as 'sly' and the community culture as 'oppressive' (Gillborn, 1992; Mac an Ghaill, 1989; and Shepherd, 1987 – all cited in Gillborn and Gipps, 1996 – and Brandt, 1986).

More recently, a study of Asian students in central Birmingham found an increase in permanent exclusions of Asian pupils, and identified problematic and conflictual relationships between Asian students and their teachers (Mehra, 1998). Excluded students reported feeling that they had been discriminated against. Bhavnani et al. (1986) found that both Black and Asian pupils felt that their teachers' treatment of them was 'subhuman'; their expectations of them low; and that the education system promoted a sense of Black and Asian cultural inferiority. Figures from a DfEE Youth Cohort Study in 2001, show that while the achievements of Black African pupils at GCSE level are currently rising faster than those of their white peers, there is hardly any increase at all in attainment levels of Pakistani pupils, and that of Bangladeshi pupils is actually falling.

However, a 1999 OFSTED survey into school and LEA practice found that on the whole, few mechanisms to address discrimination in school are yet in place. Although schools or LEAs may have equal opportunities or anti-racist policies, few monitor their implementation; neither do they review their curriculum and pastoral strategies to ensure that they are sensitive to minority groups. Only one-third of LEAs and very few schools monitor pupils' levels of attainment by ethnicity, so that general 'impressions or hunches' about the performance of different groups remain unchallenged, reinforcing stereotypes.

It is not clear to what extent the discrimination which Black and Asian pupils encounter within the education system arises out of 'unwitting' (Macpherson, 1999:28) as opposed to conscious prejudice. However an OFSTED survey of excluded minority ethnic pupils in 1996 reported this group of young people to have less severe social, family or academic problems than their white peers, indicating the contribution of in-school factors to the disproportionately high rates of ethnic minority exclusions.

Although there has been a great focus on pupil-teacher relationships, researchers have also sought explanations elsewhere. Parsons' quantitative study (1999) found that social factors, such as poverty, played a considerable role in determining exclusion rates from schools. Schaechter et al. (2000) point out the likely part played by the socio-economic position of households in educational underachievement and the difficulties experienced by schools in deprived areas. Likewise Searle (1994) and Castle and Parsons (1997) have drawn attention to the 'market system' of education created by the Education Reform Act (1988) (Searle, 1994:17) and its effects particularly on schools in disadvantaged areas. Castle and Parsons point out that the schools in these areas, suffering falling rolls, may experience greater difficulties because they are obliged to accept more difficult pupils excluded from other schools. OFSTED's (1996) study of secondary schools also found that headteachers in such schools feel under pressure to be seen to be taking a hard line in discipline and this also contributes to high exclusion rates.

Of particular interest is a recent study by Sewell (2000) where Year 10 African-Caribbean young people across different socio-economic backgrounds, regions, genders and abilities were asked what they consider to be their biggest barrier to learning in school. Eighty per cent reported this to be peer group pressure. Their teachers also identified this as a key factor in deterring them from trying hard in school. This mirrors previous findings by Sewell (1997) and Gillborn (1990) that by their efforts, high achieving Black pupils may sacrifice the goodwill of their peer group. It also falls in line with findings from a study of African American adolescents which reported that boys tended to identify low-achieving peers as admirable, and not to value high-achievers (conversely, the role models valued by the girls were largely high-achieving peers) (Graham, Taylor and Hudley, 1998). In the light of this, Sewell (2000) argues that while racism within the school system partially explains the difficulties Black pupils experience, a significant role is also played by a strong anti-school peer culture, linked to a powerful Black youth culture and its appropriation by consumer culture. He points out the dearth of research into this controversial area, and calls for Black pupils' needs around these complex issues to be more effectively addressed.

EXCLUSION – THE COSTS

In 1998/99 about 10,300 pupils were permanently excluded from school (DfEE 2000); that is, 14 in every 10,000 children. This is not a large proportion of the school age population, even allowing that official figures fail to take into account unofficial or informal exclusions, whereby a pupil is sent out of lessons by teachers or parents voluntarily remove their child when formal exclusion is imminent (Osler, 1997). However, the costs and consequences of exclusion both individually and collectively are considerable.

Exclusion is damaging and distressing for young people and carers, and reinforces feelings of disaffection (Commission for Racial Equality, 1996; Parsons and Castle, 1998). Those affected are often already experiencing other major stresses, such as family breakdown, abuse, disability or special needs (Hayden 1997). Exclusion therefore causes further difficulties, which may in turn create longer-term demands on public services (Parsons 1999; Commission for Racial Equality, 1996). Primary aged children may experience particular social and developmental repercussions, for example as a result of difficulty in successfully reintegrating into their peer group (Hayden, 1996; Hayden and Ward, 1996).

Given poor alternative educational provision for excluded young people (Audit Commission, 1999) the impact of exclusion on educational achievement is likely to be disastrous (Blyth and Milner, 1993). It has been estimated that between 70 and 80 per cent of permanently excluded youngsters fail to return to the mainstream system (Parsons, 1995; Commission for Racial Equality, 1996). Young people who miss school are more likely to be unemployed at age 18 (DfEE, 1995). Furthermore, in a survey of excluded young people, the overwhelming majority of participants disclosed some kind of offence (Graham and Bowling, 1995); and nearly half of young offenders in an Audit Commission study had been previously excluded from school (Audit Commission, 1996).

In terms of public cost, a study of six LEAs estimated each exclusion to cost education services over £4,000 a year, with costs rising if the child is still excluded the following year (Commission for Racial Equality, 1996). This is over twice the cost of mainstream schooling and includes replacement educational services at only 10 per cent of normal school time. By contrast, the cost of extra resources to support a child in full-time schooling is estimated at only £2,815. Furthermore, research has shown that this does not take into account the cost of social services care, at about £1000 a year, that one fifth of excluded young people require; or the cost of police attention, at about £2000 a year, that one quarter of excluded pupils have been found to require (Commission for Racial Equality, 1996). Using these figures, Parsons (1999) estimates that public expenditure on permanent exclusions rose in 1993/94 from about £53 million to nearly £77 million in 1997/98.

A COMMUNITY-BASED RESPONSE

The Black Community Education, Advocacy and Advice Scheme (BCEAAS) is a Bristol-based project which works to reduce the number of Black pupils (African, Caribbean and Black other) excluded from school. It was formed four years ago via a partnership between Barnardo's and the Black Communities Education Support Group (BCESG), a Black parent support group set up in inner-city Bristol in 1988 principally to recruit, train and support Black school governors.

During the late eighties and nineties, BCESG had been increasingly approached by Black parents with specific concerns about the problems their children were experiencing in school. Demand for support became greater than the organisation's limited resources could meet. Staff at a Barnardo's project in the same area were also becoming aware of these problems, though their remit and level of engagement with the Black community restricted their ability to address the issues.

Negotiations took place between the two agencies for about a year before partnership was agreed and in 1997, the Co-ordinator, Administrator and Advocacy Worker for the new service were appointed. Specific mechanisms were put in place to ensure that neither BCESG's autonomy, nor its credibility with the Black community were jeopardised by the development of the partnership. These included:

■ a consultation carried out by BCESG with their members to find out whether a new focus on support around exclusions was a priority area of work for them

■ setting up clear boundaries around the remit of the new service. BCESG continued to focus on recruitment of Black governors and other services to support Black parents, while the new service concentrated exclusively on issues around school exclusion

- although the Co-ordinator, Administrator and Advocacy Worker at the new service are paid and employed by Barnardo's, the recruitment process was primarily led by BCESG and the majority of people on the interview panel – which included both Barnardo's and BCESG staff – were Black. Posts were advertised in the local Black media, including on a local Black radio station, as well as the local and national press

- lines of accountability were established on both sides. The new service's Co-ordinator is line-managed both by the appointed link person at BCESG – in turn elected by the management committee – and also by a Barnardo's Assistant Director of Children's Services. Three-way joint management meetings are held regularly. Additionally, the new Service Co-ordinator reports to the BCESG management committee on a monthly basis. The members of this management committee are elected annually from the local Black community

- the work plan of this service is jointly owned. Although it fits in with Barnardo's wider organisational plans and targets, work is negotiated at a local level within the partnership

- both BCESG and its new service retain strong links with other local Black agencies. They also host an annual award ceremony to highlight the achievements of pupils from the Black community, which is covered extensively in the local media

Since 1997, the new service – The Black Communities Education, Advocacy and Advice Scheme (BCEAAS) – has had nearly 250 referrals of pupils from both primary and secondary schools within the old Avon authority boundaries. Key objectives for the project's work include providing support to parents of Black children in fixed-term and permanent exclusion meetings, special educational needs tribunals and admissions appeals; and negotiating reintegration of excluded youngsters into mainstream education or finding alternative provision for them. Between April 1999 and March 2000 the project saw 89 children, of whom two-thirds were boys and over half were Black African or African-Caribbean. Most referrals centred around exclusions (fixed-term and permanent) and admissions appeals. However a number of pupils were also referred for general support and advice on behaviour issues, issues with school staff or concerns around school transfers. On a strategic level, the scheme carries out interagency work with the LEA to assist in the development of education policies and has been integral in the development of the Education Action Zone anti-racist strategy in Bristol Central.

Such has been the advocacy scheme's success in retaining community credibility, that demand for services continues to outstrip project resources. The Project Co-ordinator identifies a need to target and develop services for Asian children, particularly in the light of findings on the experiences of young Asian pupils at schools. Currently only about a quarter of service users are Asian.

Through much of its support and advocacy work, the scheme helps parents and pupils manage the prejudice which they encounter within the school system. However, the scheme also works towards promoting a positive pro-learning peer culture for pupils. Resources permitting, staff hope to develop a groupwork and peer support scheme for excluded pupils; and the annual award ceremony for Black pupils also promotes a culture of working hard in school.

The central theme of the annual award ceremony is to recognise 'success in the face of adversity', an accolade of which the advocacy scheme itself is worthy. For until very recently, many schools were defensive about the difficulties experienced by their ethnic minority pupils and distrustful of engaging with Black community representatives to tackle the problem. However, the Co-ordinator at BCEAAS reports that recent years have seen a shift towards a more open working approach. To some extent this has been facilitated by Government initiatives to encourage schools to engage with issues around rising levels of exclusion (DfEE, 1998; DfEE, 1999). However at local level it has also arisen out of BCEAAS' particular success in building positive working relationships with both local schools and with the education services while at the same time retaining the trust of the local community: truly a success worthy of recognition.

REFERENCES

Audit Commission (1996) *Misspent Youth: Young People and Crime*, Audit Commission Publications

Audit Commission (1999) *Missing Out: LEA Management of School Attendance and Exclusion,*. Audit Commission Publications

Bhavnani R., Coke J., Gilroy P., Hall S., Ousley H. and Vaz K. (1986) *A Different Reality: Report of the Review Panel*, West Midlands County Council, Birmingham.

Blyth E. and Milner J. (1993) 'Exclusion from school: a first step in exclusion from society?' *Children and Society*, **7**(3), 255-68.

4

Bourne J. (1994) Facts and figures, in Bourne J., Bridges L. and Searle C., *Outcast England: How Schools Exclude Black Children*. Institute of Race Relations, London.

Brandt G.L. (1986) *The Realisation of Anti-Racist Teaching*. The Falmer Press, Basingstoke.

Castle F. and Parsons C. (1997) 'Disruptive behaviour and exclusions from schools: redefining and responding to the problem', *Emotional Difficulties* **2(3)** pp4-11

Cohen R, Hughes M., Ashworth L. and Blair M. (1994) *Schools Out: the Family Perspective on School Exclusion*, Barnardo's and Family Service Units.

Commission for Racial Equality (1996) *Exclusion for School: The Public Cost*, Commission for Racial Equality.

DfEE (1995) *Truancy and Youth Transitions*. Youth Cohort Study, 34. DfEE

DfEE (1998): The Standards Fund 1999-2000 (*Supplement to Circular 13/98*), http://www.dfee.gov.uk/ethnic/supment.htm

DfEE (1999) *The secretary of state's guidance on pupil attendance, behaviour, exclusion and re-intergration*. (Circular No. 10/99). DfEE

DfEE (2000) 'Statistics of Education: permanent exclusions from maintained schools in England',. *National Statistics Bulletin* **10/00**, DfEE.

DfEE (2001) *Youth Cohort Study: The Activities and Experiences of 16 Year Olds: England and Wales, 2000*, http://www.dfee.gov.uk/statistics/DB/SFR

Driver G. (1997) 'Cultural competence, social power and school achievement: West Indian secondary school pupils in the West Midlands', *New Community*, **5**(4), pp353-9

Gillborn D. (1990) 'When cultural display is seen as a challenge', *Times Educational Supplement*, 30 November, p10

Gillborn D. (1992) 'Racism and education: issues for research and practice', Brown S, and Riddell S. (eds) *Class, Race and Gender in Schools: A New Agenda for Policy and Practice in Scottish Education*. Scottish Council for Research in Education, Edinburgh, with the Educational Institute of Scotland.

Gillborn D. and Drew D. (1992). '"Race", class and school effects' *New Community* **18**(4), pp551-65.

4

Gillborn D. and Gipps C. (1996) *Recent Research on the Achievements of Ethnic Minority Pupils,*. OFSTED.

Gilroy P. (2000) Between Camps: Nations, Cultures and the Allure of Race. Penguin Press, London.

Graham M. and Bowling B. (1995) *Young People and Crime*, Home Office.

Graham S., Taylor A. and Hudley C. (1998) 'Exploring achievement values among ethnic minority early adolescents', *Journal of Education Psychology*, **90**(4) pp606-620.

Hayden C. (1996) 'Primary exclusions: evidence for action' *Educational Research*, **38**(2) pp213-25.

Hayden C. (1997) 'Excluded from primary school' in *Representing Children* **9**(4) pp36-44.

Hayden C. and Ward D. (1996) 'Faces behind the figures: interviews with children excluded from primary school' *Children and Society*, **10**, pp255-66.

Kinder K., Halsey K. and Kendall S. (2000) *'Working Out Well: Effective Provision for Excluded Pupils,*. NFER, Slough.

Mac an Ghaill M. (1989) 'Coming of age in 1980s England: reconceptualising Black students' schooling experiences' *British Journal of Sociology of Education* **10**(3), pp273-86.

Macpherson W. (1999) *The Stephen Lawrence Enquiry : Report*. The Stationary Office.

Mehra H. (1998) 'The permanent exclusion of Asian pupils in secondary schools in central Birmingham', *Multicultural Teaching* **17**(1), pp42-8.

OFSTED (1996) *Exclusions From Secondary Schools*, The Stationary Office, London.

OFSTED (1999) *Raising the Attainment of Minority Ethnic Pupils: Schools and LEAs Responses*, OFSTED.

Osler A. (1997) *Exclusion From School and Racial Equality: A Report for the Commission for Racial Equality*, Commission for Racial Equality, London.

Parsons C. (1995) *Final Report to the Department for Education: National Survey of Local Education Authorities Policies and Procedures for the Identification of and Provision for Children Who Are Out of School by Exclusion or Otherwise*, Christ Church College, Canterbury.

Parsons C. (1999) *Education, Exclusion and Citizenship*. Routledge, London.

Parsons C. and Castle F. (1998) 'Trends in exclusions from school : New Labour, new approaches?' *FORUM*, **40**(1), pp11-14.

Schaechter J., Grosvenor I. and Faust A. (2000) 'Feel like I come from somewhere else: an examination of the way social exclusion impacts on African Caribbean pupils', *Education and Social Justice*, **3**(1), pp9-16.

Searle C. (1994) 'The culture of exclusion', in Bourne J., Bridges L., and Searle C., *Outcast England: How Schools Exclude Black Children*, Institute of Race Relations, London.

Sewell T. (1997) *Black Masculinities and Schooling: How Black Boys Survive Modern Schooling*, Trentham Books, Chester.

Sewell T. (2000) 'Identifying the pastoral needs of African-Caribbean students: a case of critical "antiracism"', *Education and Social Justice*, **3**(1), pp17-26.

Shepherd D. (1987) 'The accomplishment of divergence', *British Journal of Sociology of Education*, **8**(3), pp263-76.

Social Exclusion Unit (1998) *Truancy and School Exclusion: Report by the Social Exclusion Unit,*. SEU, London.

Social Exclusion Unit (2000) *National Strategy for Neighbourhood Renewal: A Report of the Policy Action Team 12: Young People*, SEU, London.

Wright C. (1986) 'School processes: an ethnographic study' in The Runnymede Trust, *Education for Some: A Summary of the Eggleston Report on the Educational and Vocational Experiences of Young Black People*, The Runnymede Trust, London.

5 Community, consultation and caution:

family support and the muslim community

Alan Coombe and Nellie Maan

INTRODUCTION

This chapter describes work within a predominantly Muslim community. We detail how initial research defined a need to develop bilingual skills in pre-school children. We illustrate how the community was consulted, how they defined their situation and how that was responded to. The chapter provides a theoretical, policy and research context for activity. We suggest that effective research and practice is underpinned by a framework rooted in systemic analysis and responsiveness to expressed need. We counsel caution in the use of 'off the shelf' solutions and definitions of culture, and emphasise both the importance of listening to service users and the discipline of a theoretical structure to make sense of what is being said, to inform and prompt action.

A THEORETICAL CONTEXT

The model informing work at Khandaani Dhek Bhal (a Barnardo's project in Yorkshire), translated to Family Centre in English, is predicated on systems theory and responsiveness to service users. This has proved a useful check against the false assumption that methods tried and tested in one context are always applicable in other settings. Equally, it has underpinned our understanding that there is as much diversity within cultures as between them: individuals make their own choices about which aspects of their culture they adhere to. We do not devalue the relevance of race or faith, but suggest that individuals are given the opportunity to state what is important to them.

It is not surprising that community consultation rarely leads to consensus. Agreeing priorities with any group requires respect of wide-ranging views and differing cultural imperatives. Methodological assumptions require similar caution. Methods regarded as relevant in one context do not necessarily have a wider applicability. The challenge is to research, evaluate and develop provision pertinent to the expressed needs of the community; to focus on outcomes while remaining attentive to the many strands which underpin an assumed consensus.

A NATIONAL POLICY CONTEXT

As part of the programme of work of the Labour Government's Social Exclusion Unit, a number of Policy Action Teams were established. The report of the Policy Action Team 12 (PAT 12) (Social Exclusion Unit, 2000) identifies some policy drivers crucial to work with socially excluded children and their families. The report seeks to identify what needs to be done to develop cost-effective preventative work with disadvantaged young people in poor neighbourhoods. It articulates two key findings upon which an action plan can be predicated:

i)   the complexity of disadvantage faced by certain groups of people such as those who grow up in care, in poverty, or in deprived neighbourhoods, or who do badly at school; and

ii)   the inadequate response young people often receive from a fragmented set of services that do not organise around their needs.

The Policy Action Team notes that education does not meet the needs of a significant minority of people disproportionately concentrated in the poorest areas. Young people within ethnic minority communities also face these problems disproportionately, not least because they live in poverty and disadvantaged neighbourhoods in addition to facing the effect of racism.

PAT 12 identifies three major shortcomings in current policy and provision:

i)   gaps in individual services

ii)   allocation of resources – far from resources being targeted on those in greatest need, research reveals that while government spending on children generally increases with increasing deprivation, there are many instances where very deprived areas have less spent on them than more affluent ones

iii)   fragmentation of policy thinking and service delivery – the absence of a 'big picture' and somebody to pull it together nationally, locally and at the level of the individual.

In the light of this report, the Prime Minister established a new Cabinet Committee on Children and Young People's Services in November 2000. The Committee, supported by a cross-cutting Children and Young People's Unit, is responsible for ensuring the coherence and success of the Government's policies on preventing poverty and disadvantage in the under-19 age group. The Committee is charged with the responsibility of ensuring that the Government's approach is based on dialogue with children, young people, their parents and those who work with them, notably organisations in the children's voluntary sector.

While the Committee and the Unit are thus ostensibly responsive to the views of children and their parents, there are other implicit drivers.

The Government is wedded to an evidence-based 'what works' agenda. This is welcome, as is the acknowledgement of the substantial research as to need that exists and the recent refinement of the deprivation indices as tools for action. However the political agenda demands quick results and, unless there is meaningful dialogue with children, there could be a tendency simply to wed evidence of need with 'what works' for the indigenous community, to produce solutions not relevant to the communities they are meant to address. We propose that evidenced need in a particular community should serve as a trigger to effect dialogue with that community to ascertain how that need should best be met. Without systemic analysis of the dynamics of a particular community and continuous dialogue with that community, services will neither be responsive to individuals, families, neighbourhoods and communities of interest, nor culturally sensitive.

A RESEARCH CONTEXT

There will be a tension between the concerns ascribed to a community and those described by it. While literature reviews demonstrate that Black family life has not been an area of much study (Ahmad, 1996), there has been some work on how parenting within ethnic minority communities is perceived by others: Sharma Ahmed has provided case examples of how social workers have focused on Asian parenting in an attempt to explain the 'cultural conflict' experienced by Asian girls (Ahmed, 1986). Waqar Ahmad reminds us that behaviour is negotiated in a complex manner and influenced by various factors, including culture, economic situation, gender, age and moral identity. We should be careful in interpreting any evidence of continuity or change in family relationships and practices. While the situation for the second generation is complex, Ahmad (1996) argues that there is no research evidence to suggest that they reject their cultural and religious values. On the whole, the second generation shows much continuity with parental traditions alongside areas of modification. A study of 200 people from ethnic minority communities in London and Luton, quoted by Ahmad (1996), concluded:

i) interviewees who held on to or developed a cultural identity and values which opposed the perceived materialism and individualism of the majority in the UK community felt they coped better with most problems

ii) this often involved reliance on community spirit and spirituality, with regular meetings and discussions. Support was also gained from family, friends and religious and cultural methods of prayer

iii) interviewees felt that individuals who have tried to adopt UK values, or to mix these with competing world views, have been more vulnerable to confusion over their cultural identities and disruption within the family

iv) respondents preferred where possible to solve problems for themselves or within their families, and to abstain from the use of statutory and mainstream voluntary family service provisions

v) most respondents expressed concern that the actions of officials, such as schoolteachers and social workers, were undermining their parental authority

vi) families were adapting to life in the UK whilst remaining within their own cultural traditions, e.g. many of the young Muslim women interviewed considered that the Holy Qur'an provides the framework for true equality between women and men.

While user involvement in the development and delivery of services has been a particular feature of social service provision in the last decade, it has a much longer pedigree in family centres, particularly those viewed as community or neighbourhood resources (Holman, 1988). However a recent study of the use of family centres by black families (Butt and Box, 1999) demonstrates that all but a minority of centres have targeted black communities through outreach. They concluded from their study that family centres are not intrinsically providers of accessible and appropriate services to black families.

This brief review of the literature cautions against assuming that off the shelf strategies are applicable to ethnic minority communities without further consultation. Research may highlight the service provision deficit but does not negate the need to actively listen to children and parents if the new services are to be responsive to real need.

THE LOCAL CONTEXT

Khandaani Dhek Bhal was established in 1996 with the aim of enhancing the educational and employment prospects of children, young people and significant adults within the Muslim community of Heckmondwike, raising awareness of local services and encouraging the take-up of such services by Asian families. The project was a consequence of research undertaken by Kirklees Early Years Service, which had highlighted a need for earlier interventions to support the development of bilingual skills in pre-school children. An assessment of English language development had indicated that two-thirds of the 6000 pupils from minority ethnic communities within targeted areas had insufficient command of English to access the National Curriculum. No schools achieved the then national average (41.1%) for the numbers of pupils attaining five or more A – C grades at GCSE. Achievement in Heckmondwike was amongst the lowest in Kirklees. While participation in full-time education was higher for young people from ethnic minority communities than for the overall population (69% compared to 64%), the evidence suggested that they were re-sitting GCSE exams or pursuing courses ranked at or below GNVQ2. Non-participation in education or employment was higher for young people from ethnic minority communities at 16% than for white young people at 11%. Contemporary work with parents in nursery and infant schools demonstrated low levels of literacy, particularly among Asian mothers.

CONSULTATION WITH THE MUSLIM COMMUNITY

The findings from the Kirklees research prompted a consultation exercise specific to the needs of Heckmondwike (Maan, 1996). This research exercise was conducted within a systems approach to understanding the needs of the Asian community and its relationship to the wider community and service providers. The consultation took the form of a 'general inquiry' (Reid and Smith, 1981). Semi-structured interviews were undertaken with community members, including a focus group with men, as well as professionals. The research revealed that there was a lack of services in Heckmondwike in general and that the services were not sensitive to the needs of the community. For example, women wanted to learn English in their own homes or at a local community centre rather than college. A need was identified for a pre-school service for children, as for many children their first experience of education was at primary school.

The resulting project effected the shift from a deficit model implicit in the original Kirklees research to one responding to and building on people's own learning, including providing a library for use by the whole community, regular community-based activities, and requests for specific services for the following groups in the community:

i)   women requested educational classes in English, First Aid and information technology together with opportunities to gain experience of the work environment through volunteering

ii)   for children, a pre-school nursery, after school and holiday clubs were requested

iii)   young people requested educational classes, residential trips (for outward bound activities, such as abseiling, canoeing, climbing etc.), mentoring and volunteering opportunities.

SYSTEMS THEORY – THEORY AND APPLICATION AT KHANDAANI DHEK BHAL

The systems model aids understanding and informs action predicated on a need to embrace 'culture' not be driven by it. Culture exists within a dynamic relationship with many other factors. The theory, while originating in cybernetics, was briefly prominent in social work in the 1970s (Pincus and Minahan, 1973) and particularly structural family therapy (Minuchin, 1974). More recently a multi-systemic approach has been revived in 'family preservation' practice in the USA (Cimmarusti, 1992). A system such as a family or community is presented as a whole, its components and characteristics only understood as functions of the total system (Walrond-Skinner, 1976).

A system may be open or closed (Hall and Fagen, 1956). Open systems are understood as those where there is a high level of communication with the environment. Few systems are completely closed or open. The construct serves to establish the extremities of a continuum on which families, communities etc. may be viewed as relatively one or the other (Ackoff, 1972). The useful, central assumption of systems theory is that every system is goal-orientated, purposive and acts to maintain its own existence irrespective of individuals' understanding of this. A system seeks to achieve homeostasis; dysfunction may be an unintended consequence of this purpose. Effective change requires that a new balance, one not characterised by dysfunction, to be achieved. The 'change system' comprises those elements, individuals, agencies, etc. that effect such change.

At Khandaani Dhek Bhal the nuclear family was understood as a system whose permeable boundaries included those with the extended family and the community, but whose relationship to education, health and social services was characterised by less than a two-way flow. To work effectively with families from the Muslim community, it was important to evaluate not only the relationship between systems comprising the wider contacts or environment, but also the project per se as a system. Family systems were strongly influenced by the community system; a relatively open relationship existed between the two systems. Thus any work with families needed to evaluate the response from and impact upon the wider community, including the Faith community, e.g. services for children after school had to take account of the expectations of the community Mosque school. Family systems were relatively closed to agencies such as schools and colleges. In approaching the local college to deliver community-based English classes for Asian women – it not being acceptable within the family system for women to attend the college itself – positive and lasting change was the goal within both the family and the educational systems.

RESPONSIVENESS TO USERS

Once the research had been conducted within the systems framework, the practice was very much influenced by the responsiveness to service users model developed by Parasuraman, Zeithaml and Berry (1985, 1988, 1991).

An emphasis on meeting customer need has grown in prominence throughout the 1990s although caution needs to be exercised if providers are not to be deluded by the rhetoric. We often at times state that we want choice when in reality we more simply want what we want, not a range of options. Thus Parasuraman, Zeithaml and Berry (1985, 1988, 1991) argue that meeting customer need is fundamentally about the provision of a quality service, i.e. 'the degree to which attributes of the service desired by the users are identified and incorporated in the service and the degree to which desired levels of these attributes are perceived by the users to be achieved' (Murdick, Render and Russell, 1990). Parasuraman, Zeithaml and Berry have identified ten attributes which customers use to assess service quality.

Characteristic	Definition
Tangibles	Appearance of physical facilities, equipment, personnel, and communication materials
Reliability	The ability to perform the service dependably and accurately
Responsiveness	Willingness to assist customers and provide a service
Competence	Having the requisite skills, knowledge and experience to perform the service
Courtesy	Being respectful and friendly to customers at all times
Credibility	Trustworthiness and honesty of service provider

Security	Freedom from danger, risk or doubt
Access	Approachability and ease of contact
Communication	Keeping customers informed in a language that they understand
Understanding the customer	Making the effort to understand what the customer really needs

Meeting customer need is therefore as much about delivery as it is about 'end product'. For example, a service may succeed in helping customers secure income support, but it is of low quality if delivered in an inaccessible venue where the service user waits at length in a smoke-filled room and once seen is subject to constant interruptions.

Khandaani Dhek Bhal started from an awareness of the cultural and religious aspects of the community it serves, but went on to determine the actions consequent on this understanding within a framework that enabled monitoring and evaluation, i.e. asking users what aspects of the service were important to them (Maan & Cooke, 1997). A focus group was convened to explore the relative importance of the ten attributes, listed above, with service users. Their responses informed the structure of a questionnaire which listed the different service characteristics valued by service users that would adequately reflect these attributes. This questionnaire was then used in another focus group to determine the percentage gap between service users' expectations (Exp) and perceptions (Per) of the various service characteristics, as detailed below.

Service Characteristic	Exp	Per	Gap	Reason/Comments
Project should look Asian	100%	25%	- 75%	The project was housed in a temporary base at the time of the research. Comments made by service users were incorporated into the design of the project base.
Staff should be polite, friendly and welcoming	100%	100%	0	Although expectations/ perceptions match, further work is needed to identify important elements.
Staff should be willing to help	100%	100%	0	High levels of communication must be maintained with service users to maintain standard.

Staff should understand Islam and the Muslim culture	95%	90%	- 5%	Staff composition (70% Muslim) contributed to this standard. The project must maintain training for all staff.
Project should open at convenient times	95%	100%	+ 5%	Operating times suit service users. However, operating times must be monitored to respond to changing needs.
Project should be locally based	95%	80%	- 15%	Although the project base is fairly central, options need to be explored to target peripheral groups, e.g. satellite work.
Project should tell people what it will do to help	95%	45%	- 50%	Many service users not informed about the work of the project. Although the project is in its infancy, steps must be taken to close the gaps.
Project should keep its promises	90%	85%	- 5%	Standards adopted by the project must be communicated to partner agencies. Systems need to be in place to manage user requests.
Staff should be trained	90%	100%	+ 10%	Perception held that staff are trained, but users not in a position to assess.
Project should guarantee safety for women	90%	95%	+ 5%	Project has ensured that men are not present during women-only sessions.
Information should be available in Urdu	85%	90%	+ 5%	The bilingual skills of staff ensure that information can be communicated verbally in Urdu.
Project should tell people what services will be provided and when	85%	45%	- 50%	The project decided not to communicate the likely service provision given the uncertainty around a permanent base. Much work now needs to be done.
Information should remain confidential	85%	85%	0%	This area needs urgent attention as both perception and expectation should be 100%.

Project should ask people what help they want	85%	90%	+ 5%	Although project does well, this must be a continuous practice.
Project should involve parents when working with their children	85%	60%	- 15%	Project works with children in schools at the request of schools. Steps need to be taken to ensure that either the schools or the project informs parents.
Staff should be respectfully dressed	70%	100%	+ 30%	Standards must be maintained in this area.
Project should tell people about their right to complain	75%	75%	0%	Further work is needed to empower service users and inform them of their rights.
Staff should speak Urdu	75%	100%	+ 25%	The importance of staff speaking Urdu cannot be overestimated.
Project should tell people that it keeps information about them Project should tell people what information it keeps about them				Scoring in area was not very relevant. Many service users were not aware that agencies keep information on users, what information is kept, and why. The project must take steps to ensure that awareness is raised.
Project should tell people how it works	60%	30%	- 30%	The project at the time of research was still in its infancy. However, it is clear that a greater level of communication is needed.
Project should ask people to complain if not happy about something	60%	80%	+ 20%	The project has worked towards empowering users with their rights. Further work is clearly needed.
Project should ask children what help they want	60%	15%	- 45%	This is partly linked with the work with children in schools. More work is needed to involve both parents and children in the decision making process on service provision.
Project should help people quickly	35%	70%	+ 35%	This perhaps reflects users' previous experiences and needs further work.

Service users' views thus revealed four areas characterised by significant shortfall of quality:

i)   tangibles – e.g. the building needs to be culturally and religiously reflective

ii)   responsiveness – a willingness to help service users with their problems and more importantly be perceived as willing to help

iii) credibility – service users' experience of other service providers has created a sense of mistrust – the project needs to work towards building its credibility through open and honest communication

iv)   communication – service users need to be told what services the project is providing when and how, as well as communicating general information about the project in a language that service users understand.

A number of steps were taken to tackle this gap. These included:

i)   the project base now reflects the cultural/religious expectations of the community, with a dedicated prayer room, appropriate images and displays

ii)   bilingual literature is available on the work of the project, its policies, procedures, rights of service users etc. All new service users are informed of how the project works and given an information pack. Essential policies are available in Urdu and audio tape. The establishment of an active service users' committee and the recruitment of local volunteers has enabled the project to become well known within the area

iii) all new service users are informed about the organisation's recording policies. In some instances, service users have decided not to use the service

iv)   it is now standard practice to consult both children and parents as well as those agencies requesting the service before any work commences. Regular reviews and feedback questionnaires ensure that the work is continuously relevant to the identified needs.

The project exceeded service users' expectations of quality in the remaining six areas namely, competence, courtesy, access, security, reliability and understanding. The framework, however, checks against complacency by facilitating sampling of practice and continuous review, e.g. a summer playscheme was seen not to meet the need vocalised by service users; a summer school requested by service users did meet that need the following year. Service design, delivery and evaluation continue under the aegis of a service users' committee, which works to a participative rather than empowering agenda, thus maintaining the momentum of the original consultative exercise.

CONCLUSION

It is suggested in this chapter that Khandaani Dhek Bhal exemplifies the proposition that an equalities agenda is best delivered if it is informed by systemic analysis and characterised by responsiveness to the expressed views of service users.

Such analysis provides an understanding that cannot be otherwise gained by aggregating knowledge of diverse cultures. Listening to people checks assumptions that could otherwise skew understanding of cultural imperatives. Far better that we emphasise the choices individuals make within their cultural environment rather than the cultural milieu itself.

REFERENCES

Ackoff R.L. (1972) 'Towards a system of systems concepts', in Beishon J. and Peters G., *Systems Behaviour*, Open University Press, London.

Ahmed S. (1986) 'Asian girls and social workers', in Ahmed S. Cheetham J. and Small J. *Social Work With Black Children and Their Families*, British Agencies for Adoption & Fostering.

Ahmad W.I.U. (1996) 'Black family life, in Ahmad W.I.U. and Atkin K. (eds) *'Race' and Community Care*, Open University Press, Buckingham.

Butt J. and Box L. (1999) 'Family centred: a study of the use of family centres by black families; *Research Policy and Planning*, **17** (3), pp14-15.

Butt J. and Phillips M. (1996) 'Enquiries into allegations: a black perspective, in Platt D. and Shemmings D. (eds) *Making Enquiries into Alleged Child Abuse and Neglect: Partnership with Families*, Pennant, Brighton.

Cimmarusti R. (1992) 'Family preservation practice based upon a multisystems approach', *Child Welfare*, **71** (3), May-June, pp241-256.

Hall A.D. and Fagen R.E. (1956) 'Definition of system' in Bertalanffy L. von and Rappaport A. (eds) *General Systems Yearbook 1* Society of General Systems Research.

5

Holman B. (1988) Putting Families First: Prevention and Child Care: A Study of Prevention by Statutory and Voluntary Agencies, Macmillan Education, Basingstoke.

Maan N. (1996) Heckmondwike Project: Research Paper, Barnardo's.

Maan N. and Cooke H. (1997) *A Study of Customer Expectations and Perceptions of Quality of Services Provided by a Barnardo's Project: a Market Research Module for the MBA Course at the Bradford Management Centre.*

Minuchin S. (1974) *Families and Family Therapy*, Tavistock Publications, London.

Murdick R.G., Render B. and Russell R.S. (1990) *Service Operations Management*, Allyn and Bacon, Boston.

Parasuraman A. Zeithaml V.A. and Berry L.L. (1985) 'A conceptual model of service quality and its implications for future research', *Journal of Marketing*, **49** (4), Fall, pp41-50.

Parasuraman A. Zeithaml V.A. and Berry L.L. (1988) 'SERVQUAL: A multiple-item scale for measuring consumer perceptions of service quality', *Journal of Retailing*, **64**, (1), Spring, pp12-40.

Parasuraman A., Berry L.L. and Zeithaml V.A. (1991) 'Refinement and reassessment of the SERVQUAL scale', *Journal of Retailing*, **67** (4), Winter, pp420-450.

Pincus A. and Minahan A. (1973) *Social Work Practice: Model and Method*, Peacock, Itasca, Illinois.

Reid W.J. and Smith A.D. (1981) *Research in Social Work*. Columbia University Press.

Social Exclusion Unit (2000) *National Strategy for Neighbourhood Renewal: A Report of the Policy Action Team 12: Young People*, Social Exclusion Unit, London.

Walrond-Skinner S. (1976) Family Therapy: The Treatment of Natural Systems, Routledge and Kegan, Paul, London.

To attach and belong: 6

Scotland's black children in family placement

Satnam Singh, Sue Macfadyen and Angie Gillies

INTRODUCTION: BARNARDO'S SERVICE WITHIN THE SCOTTISH CONTEXT

Family Placement Services (FPS) is an adoption and fostering project based in Edinburgh, which specialises in providing substitute families for children who are unable to live at home. Some of these children are Black or of a Black mixed parentage. However, given that the Black population in Scotland is around 2%, the numbers of Black children requiring placement will always be low, and much lower than in England where the Black population is around 6-7%. As a result of these demographics, the needs of minority ethnic communities in Scotland have not been viewed as a priority and have been overlooked in many areas of public service. Only recently, with the publication of the Macpherson report (1999) has there been an open acknowledgement of the existence of racism in British public institutions. The Macpherson report highlights the need for public institutions to analyse policy and practice with regard to equal delivery in services, and states:

> It is incumbent upon every institution to examine their policies and the outcome of their policies and practices to guard against disadvantaging any section of our communities (Macpherson, 1999).

The 1991 census suggested that 1.3% of the Scottish population identified itself as being from a minority ethnic community (OPCS, 1993). Bowes and Sim (1991) point out, that however, this general picture conceals local concentrations of Black people, principally in the urban centres of Glasgow and Edinburgh, where that figure is thought to be closer to 3-4%. A similar demographic trend may be found in some areas of England and Wales, where the Black and minority ethnic populations are low, in comparison to larger urban populations such as Birmingham or Bradford. In terms of social services provision, this has recently been cause for greater attention and concern, as research (BEMIS, 1999) indicates that most Scottish local authorities have minimised the needs of Black communities and individuals, justifying this on the basis of low numbers.

Studies particular to Scotland for example, document a very low awareness among social work managers of statutory duties under the 1976 Race Relations Act (Cadman and Chakrabarti, 1991). This results in what McCluskey (1991) observes as 'a non-White population, which is expected to "fit in" with existing (White) services'. In this respect, the overall situation in Scotland may reflect the conditions in some of the more rural authorities in England and Wales.

Within social work, the Children (Scotland) Act 1995 introduced the concept of paying due 'regard to a child's racial origin, religious persuasion and cultural and linguistic background', a concept that had been introduced six years earlier in England through the 1989 Children Act. This has been acknowledged by the Social Work Services Inspectorate (SWSI) in its 1998 document, Valuing Diversity, which states in its preface:

> In addressing their needs (Black children) it is important to take account of their individual characteristics. Race, culture, language and religion are amongst the most important of these (Scottish Office, 1998)

Some social workers in Scotland had been acting in accordance with this principle prior to the 1995 Act. However, there had been little in terms of guidance which had supported or empowered them in promoting and meeting such needs. The 1995 Act, and its accompanying guidance, therefore, has been a significant milestone in the provision of services to Scotland's Black communities, in that the specific duties to identify, assess and meet the needs of Black and minority ethnic children are now enshrined in social work statute.

The invisibility of Black children in Scotland, coupled with the competing demands on local authority resources, has contributed to the low priority given to the need to recruit foster carers and adoptive parents from a range of ethnic backgrounds.

For example, in 1999, the Scottish Office funded a high profile media campaign to recruit foster carers within local authorities, but did not focus on recruiting minority ethnic carers. The Scottish Office guidance to L.As on implementing the Children (Scotland) Act 1995 states that '...background should be catered for within placement, with carers, or one or more staff members sharing the child's religion and heritage', yet within their own recruitment campaign it was decided that as services for minority ethnic groups were being developed by Barnardo's, local authority recruitment should focus on their greater demand – white Scottish children. Black children who become looked after and accommodated cannot then benefit from same-race placement in their own locality and community unless the local authority purchases the service offered by Barnardo's Family Placement Services – the Khandan Initiative. Local authorities facing competing demands for finance are choosing to place children transracially. This clearly illustrates the struggle faced by both practitioners and agencies to give equal priority to the needs of Black children.

The position in England is slightly different, particularly in the areas of high Black population. The 'Soul kids' campaign in the 1970s, whilst not successful in recruiting many families, influenced the development of similar strategic campaigning by some of the inner city London Boroughs. Driven by some early successes, and the efforts of ABSWAP (Association of Black Social Workers and Allied Professions), the principles and practices of same-race placements for Black children are now much more clearly embedded into the 'routine thinking' and professional discourse around Black children's needs and are evidenced in some local authorities' achievements in making appropriate placements (Barn, 1993). However, without the added 'weight' of higher population densities, as in Scotland or the rural authorities in England and Wales, creating and sustaining a higher profile for looked after Black children has proved more difficult.

This background shapes the context within which we will examine the development of the Khandan Initiative, a specific service developed by FPS for minority ethnic children. The aim of the Khandan Initiative is to provide same-race placements as placements of choice.

To begin, however, we will discuss the theoretical frameworks that inform family placement work. To help substantiate this discussion we reviewed the case files of six Black children who had been transracially placed by Barnardo's family placement services over the last decade or so. Throughout the rest of this paper we will be drawing on some of these cases as a way of illustrating our discussion.

REVIEWING THE THEORY: TO ATTACH...

One of the key theoretical underpinnings of family placement work is that of attachment, and perhaps more recently that of resilience. By its very nature, permanent family placement involves the severing of primary attachments for children and the fostering of new attachments with substitute carers or adoptive parents. This psychological process, being both complex and highly variable, is still not fully understood. As is pointed out in the 1992 report issued by the World Health Organisation:

> Though more has recently been learnt about how it [attachment] operates, much more work is still needed concerning its aetiology, how to recognize it and how to measure its strength (World Health Organisation, 1992).

6

Despite such complexity, and in the face of the emotional intensity that surrounds the plight of children who cannot live with their own families, the emphasis on attachment provides a context and focus to all involved in the process of placement.

Although some of the early work on attachment was undertaken in Uganda (Ainsworth et al. 1978), many of the main ideas arising from John Bowlby's seminal work on attachment, separation and loss (1969) were developed within a white European/American framework and mindset. Attachment theory assumes to a great extent that children share the culture, race, religion and language of the wider community. As a result, attachment theory does not fully consider the needs of Black children within the context of a white society, nor indeed the impact of racism on these children.

In the main, attachment theory has been used to provide an understanding both of the child's emotional needs and behaviour, and also of the bonding processes that occur in adoption and permanent fostering (e.g. Howe, 1995). In this respect attachment theory does indeed make significant and valuable contributions to the understanding of separation and loss and the impact of this on children's development. However, many of the 'taken for granted' concepts of attachment theory still hold very clear Eurocentric biases. For example one of the leading proponents of attachment theory, Vera Fahlberg, emphasises the importance of balancing dependency with autonomy, but fails to recognize the diversity that exists in Black families, where the notion of interdependence is a much more central feature. Gambe et al. (1992) write that much of Fahlberg's 'attachment checklists' requires social workers to judge what is 'normal, appropriate, and/or positive'. They highlight the following example from Fahlberg (1981):

Do(es) the parent(s) -

> Use **appropriate** disciplinary measures?
>
> Comfort the child in a **positive** way?
>
> Initiate **positive** interaction with the child?
>
> Accept expressions of **autonomy?**

Gambe et al. point out that each of these judgements will be likely to be based on Eurocentric assumptions unless workers take account of the racial and cultural context whilst making assessments. Singh (1997) suggests that 'assessments should ... be drawn from the (child's) social and cultural milieu'.

Attachment theory in itself, therefore, does not fully address the wider issues of identity and identity development, which are of considerable significance for Black children. These wider processes of identity formation arise partly through a connection with primary attachment figures and partly through a shared experience of language, community, religion, history, and culture. It is important therefore that planning for Black children should draw on the significant contributions of the attachment theorists, while also challenging the underlying assumptions about identity formation that are subsumed or overlooked in traditional placement practice.

REVIEWING THE THEORY: TO BELONG...

As early as 1979, identity formation and identity maintenance were seen as a significant task for all children in substitute care:

> The child who must be placed in substitute care at any age, and regardless of the reason, is torn from the biological and symbolic context of his identity. No matter how nurturing the substitute care, the child's ongoing task will always be to reweave the jagged tear in the fabric of his identity, to make himself whole again.
> (Germaine, 1979: 175-6)

However, this issue of identity has been overlooked or relegated to a lesser consideration for many Black children, resulting in their being placed transracially into white substitute families. Consequently the task of 'reweaving' the fabric of their identity is made all the more difficult.

Owusu-Bempah and Howitt (1997) introduce the idea of a socio-genealogical connectedness, which emphasizes the aspect of children identifying with their natural parents' biological and social backgrounds. It refers to the way in which a child sees him/herself as part of his/her parents' background both in a biological and in a sociological sense, and suggests that identity includes a need to feel 'connected to heritage and biological roots' (Owusu-Bempah and Howitt, 1997:204) in addition to the emotional bonding and development provided through attachment.

Even where a child has secure attachments with primary caregivers, this in itself is not sufficient to give the child a sense of wholeness, or a sense of completeness. 'Bonding without a sense of racial identity is pathological and is against the best interest of the Black child' (ABSWAP, 1983). Studies have shown that children can indeed maintain good self-esteem but have no sense of their core identity (Tizzard and Pheonix, 1993).

A sense of wholeness comes also from connection to family and community that reflects back experiences of sameness and belonging. This process is likely to be much

6

more difficult and incomplete for black children placed transracially into predominantly white communities.

Similarly, Howe (1995) suggests that many adult transracial adoptees report that, once they leave home, they feel that they do not belong anywhere. On the one hand they are not fully accepted in the White community and – even though they are more accepted in the Black community – they often do not understand various cultural nuances. Race and culture cannot be ignored. As Howe (1995) has noted:

> The key to successful living as a minority person in a discriminatory, denigrating society is to have positive affirmation with others like oneself, from whom one can gain support and affirmation and learn coping skills.

The interactionist theories of Cooley (1902) and Mead (1934), offer the proposal of the development of self-concept through the idea of a 'looking glass self'. According to Cooley (1902):

> What an organism internalized as his own was based on information about oneself which is received from others (cited in Nobles, 1973).

Similarly, Mead (1934) saw the development of 'I' and 'Me' as the perception of oneself as reflected by the shared meanings and values of 'others'. Both these ideas are developed by Nobles (1973) in relation to the Black self-concept, which he suggests has to consider the notion of 'We', as well as the 'I' and 'Me'. This 'We', is the sense of belonging which manifests in the feelings and attitudes towards the group and by the group. More recently, Banks (1997) writes that an integrated Black identity has to include a positive and balanced view and attitude about one's own group.

A secure sense of identity arises not just from attachment relationships, but from biological and social connectedness, which together provide 'psychological integrity ....who we are, what we want to be, where we come from and where we belong in the order of things' (Owusu-Bempah and Howitt, 1997:201). Some evidence for this can be seen in the need for some adult adoptees to search for their birth relatives or parents, with whom an emotional relationship no longer actively exists, even when securely attached to their adoptive family.

Socio-genealogical connectedness, then, has some important contributions to our understanding of the wider identity needs that are required for children in foster and adoptive placements, some of which may only be available through information about (and contact with) the natural family. These wider identity needs – precarious enough for children who cannot grow up in their own families, where the biological connection has been severed – are unlikely to be met in transracial placements, where the sense of racial, cultural and historical connectedness is also eroded.

For Black children, this problem is further complicated and compounded by the experience of racism, which perpetuates alienation and further demeans and devalues their identity and difference. In the small survey of transracial placements reviewed for this paper, there are frequent references to the child being singled out, stared at and verbally abused in the local white community. Children have tried to cope with such racism by denying who they are, or by attempting to change the way they look by trying to alter their skin or hair colour, or at least, by adopting a 'white' name. This is an effort to feel as if they 'fit in' or are accepted. This process of Black children responding to racism is not limited to transracial placements, and to some lesser extent is a feature of the Black child's development into adulthood within the context of a predominantly white environment. What is perhaps more disturbing is that the children within a 'looked after' situation feel that they need to change their skin colour, in order to fit in and be accepted, despite having a range of qualified professionals responsible for their welfare. The true impact of such experiences on the Black child within a transracial placement may be minimised or discounted by the white adults around him or her.

The dilemmas about identity which, a transracial placement poses for a young person are potentially huge, particularly in the context of racism. If the emphasis of the placement, however subtle, is on assimilation, then the fact of racism will have to be denied even as it is experienced by the young person. If the emphasis is on celebrating and giving equal value to cultural diversity, then the separation of the young person from her/his culture through the transracial placement cuts across this valuing. Either way, the young person is left to struggle with these fundamental splits in identity.

Consequently, the use of attachment theory to support transracial placements takes for granted or even misinterprets the wider issues of shared cultural and racial history which contribute significantly to identity and a sense of value and belonging. In the cases we surveyed for this paper, we found that there was often confusion for workers around integrating the different aspects of a Black child's identity, with emphasis frequently given to a child's socialisation into the white community or into the 'Scottish culture'.

This kind of approach makes a transracial placement seem all the more acceptable but denies the reality that the child carries, of his or her racial difference. Racial origin should not, therefore, be an optional extra in a long list of criteria for a placement, but is fundamental and central to a child's identity and experience.

6 REVIEWING THE THEORY: INTRODUCING RESILIENCE...

The recent studies on resilience in childcare also provide some other support for widening the focus away from the exclusive domain of attachment as the main factor in healthy development.

Resilience is defined by Gilligan as:

> *qualities which cushion a vulnerable child from the worst effects of adversity in whatever form it takes and which may help a child or young person to cope, survive and even thrive in the face of great hurt and disadvantage* (Gilligan, 1997:12).

He offers a perspective which recognises the importance of primary attachment figures but also highlights the benefits to the child of other relationships and resources which can serve to boost a child's individual resilience. He argues that 'social and cultural competence for children in or out of care – derives ultimately from a child's sense of belonging to a social network reflecting familial, school, neighbourhood, ethnic and cultural elements' (Gilligan, 1997:14). This complements the idea of 'socio-genealogical connectedness' which proposes that we consider the whole child being connected to his or her racial, cultural and historical origins.

Daniel, Wassell and Gilligan (1999) list six core elements in fostering resilience. These are: a secure base, education, friendships, talents and interests, positive values and social competence. For Black children placed in Black families, there may be many opportunities to build resilience from within a protective environment of community and religious organisations, for example, participation in prayer or play groups within a Mosque or within extended family networks. They may experience adult modelling of strong and positive value systems, and social relationships, and experience a sense of responsibility towards family.

We would suggest that young Black people need the opportunity to build self-esteem and an understanding of their own power and control by experiencing positive relationships that value their identity, ethnicity and background. This is best provided within a Black family that can offer these possibilities for developing resilience. Black children in Scotland, and in areas of England where Black populations may be low, have the additional task of constructing a positive identity and developing resilience within a predominately white society.

Daniel, Wassell and Gilligan (1999) describe school as providing a complementary secure base to home, a place where young people can find positive contact with peers and supportive adults. It is important to consider the environment of the school and whether such role models exist for young Black people. Research into the use of Black mentors in education (Robinson and West, 1999) provides support to the idea of introducing relevant and significant Black adults who could provide 'connectedness' for Black children in a system which might be lacking in appropriate role models.

REVIEWING THE PRACTICE: ANTI-RACISM OR PRAGMATISM

The arguments for and against same-race placements have long been debated (summarised in Smith and Berridge, 1993), with research evidence often apparently leading to differing conclusions. This in itself has perhaps contributed to the common situation in agencies where same-race placements are supported in principle, but transracial placements in particular cases are not ruled out, usually on the grounds of a pre-existing attachment or a lack of same-race resources. While this pragmatism may be understandable, given the absence of definitive research evidence and given the very emotive and high profile of the issue within the media and government, it is our contention that such a pragmatic approach can perpetuate the lack of focus on, and investment in, the recruitment of foster carers and adoptive parents from minority ethnic groups. However, in all the prolonged and recurring debates concerning same-race placements, it is salutary to remember that the vast majority of transracial placements are of black children placed with white families. This fact points to the heart of the matter, and demonstrates what Skellington and Morris (1992) call the 'racially ordered' nature of society, where access to wealth, employment, social services and even justice is determined to some degree by race. By virtue of their colour, many black children are denied access to foster parents of the same race. Put bluntly, transracial placements as they mostly occur, are a symptom of the inequality and discrimination that lie behind racism. In a letter to the Caribbean Times, David Divine wrote passionately that this one-way trafficking of black children into white families was the modern day equivalent of slavery. These children, he wrote, are:

> ...Lost to our communities. No community can afford hundreds of such casualties each year, no community can be so profligate with its most precious resources – it's children. (Divine, 1983).

This inequality was perhaps masked by ideals of integration and multiculturalism that originally supported the development of transracial placements in the 1960s and 1970s. (Smith and Berridge, 1993:17). However, as the conceptions and assumptions of multiculturalism have increasingly come to be challenged, (e.g. Cohen and Baines, 1998; Singh et al. 2000) so the inadequacy of this approach to transracial placements has also been exposed. Ideas and proclamations of multiculturalism 'assume [an] equality that defines racism away rather than dealing with it and obscures the necessity of...

confront[ing] racism as a structural inequality and endemic feature of society'
(Dominelli, 1998: 55). The fact of there even being a 'need' to justify same-race
placements for Black children reveals the covert and often unaware nature of
structural and institutional racism. Thus, ensuring that same-race placements are as
available to Black children as they are to white children is not just about good
practice, but also about actively addressing the inertia and assumptions that
perpetuate institutional racism.

BLACK CHILDREN IN SCOTLAND: A HIDDEN NEED

In Scotland, the identity needs of Black children have, to some extent, been ignored or
underplayed by adoption and fostering agencies, resulting in very few carers from
Black or minority ethnic communities. The lower profile of race issues tended to be
equated with either an absence of need or even of racism (Gilroy, 1987). During the
early 1990s attempts were made by the main social work authorities in Scotland at
recruiting Black and Asian carers. Anecdotal evidence, however, would suggest that
these efforts were hard to sustain, mainly due to a lack of resources. Basic practice
such as ethnic monitoring has been patchy at best (Singh et al. 2000), with this lack of
fundamental information contributing to the erratic or non-existent nature of a service
for Black children. BAAF Scotland recognised the need to create a higher profile and
status around recruiting Black carers, and has appointed a part-time Black consultant
to provide guidance and impetus to meeting the needs of Black children who are
accommodated.

Within Barnardo's Family Placement Services (FPS) in the early 1990s, attention was
also drawn to the needs of Black children because of a sudden increase in referrals.
Within a period of about 12 months, the project made six transracial placements, all
initially on a short-term basis. However, all but two of these converted to permanency.
The reasons for the transracial nature of these placements and the subsequent
conversion to permanency can be gleaned from the contemporary case recordings,
which highlight a number of significant issues. First, a lack of same-race resources.
Agencies had not recruited ethnically diverse placement opportunities at this time.
Second, these children had already spent a lengthy time within a white care system
and were seen or saw themselves as white. This denial of Black identity could
particularly be seen in the way practitioners argued for respecting white Scottish
origins in Black children of mixed parentage background. The subsequent transracial
placements did not offer opportunity for connectedness to their Black Asian origins.

Additional arguments centred around the attachments already made in transracial
placements and the children themselves requesting placements within a white family.
There did not seem to be any assessment of the process of denial that was leading
children to make such requests. It would appear that balancing the needs of children

who had been waiting for families with the potential resources required to recruit specific carers, led to an expediency approach to placement.

Acting positive: anti-racism in practice

The history of these referrals reflects the wider state of services for Black children in Scotland requiring family placement, and reveals the importance of the guidance to the Children (Scotland) Act (1995), which has done much since it was issued to heighten awareness of this area of practice and service provision. These children, who were all referred initially for bridge or short-term fostering, were all placed transracially with white foster families, because of an absence of Black carers. Until this time, little thought or emphasis had been given to meeting the needs of Black children by the project, despite its high profile as the main specialist placement agency in Scotland. For the majority of these children, the plans over the initial 6-18 months changed to permanence rather than a return home. Even after this time, no Black carers had been recruited by the project, despite a growing awareness of the importance of same-race placements, which was the stated policy for Barnardo's as a whole. As a result, several of these transracial placements became permanent or long-term, for which an 'exceptional circumstance' clause within Barnardo's policy was invoked.

The very existence of such 'justificatory' clauses adds to the inertia around setting the proper groundwork and resources for recruiting Black carers. This fact was well appreciated by the project, which found itself in the awkward and complex position of making and supporting transracial placements that cut across its own stated policies. Arising from this paradoxical situation, the project established a working group to look at what would be required in order to overcome the inertia and assumptions that resulted in a failure to prioritise and recruit same-race carers for Black children. One of the main outcomes of this group was an awareness of the need for much more actively anti-racist practices to counter the racism – subtle as well as institutional – that had led to the transracial placements. Having a policy statement is one thing, but translating it into action and practice that results in same-race placements for all children is quite another.

Developing the service – the Khandan Initiative

Part of the challenge lay in recognising the implications of the project having always been an all-white team, with the attitudes, perspectives and 'blindspots' that arise from that. Hence, the lack of impetus to achieving same-race placements arose because it was never quite accorded quite the priority it required, not in terms of ideals, but in terms of actual awareness, resources and direct application. As this reality came to be accepted, so the need to incorporate a Black anti-racist perspective took priority.

It was from an awareness of this need that FPS began to develop strategies through which both individuals and the project could progress towards anti-racist practice. "Anti-racist" practice is entirely different from being "ethnically sensitive", being aware of "cultural issues", or even giving due consideration to racial origin, religious persuasion, cultural or linguistic background. It assumes a level of awareness, an understanding of how racism operates in wider society, within and between agencies, structures and procedures and on an individual level between worker and family (Wilson, 1991:15).

Anti-racist practice then, does not emerge until workers examine their institutional practices that disadvantage Black children and families and take account of the power issues in wider society which affect decision making about children. Nobles (1978) sums this up powerfully:

> *One's ability to understand Black reality is limited if the interpretative framework for that reality is based on assumptions associated with a non-Black reality.*

In recognising the need to open up a wider perspective, recruiting a Black worker became the next step. FPS was able to secure funding from the Scottish Office for the costs involved in the employment and support of a Black worker for an initial two-year period. The aim of this post was to take a lead role in helping the project develop its anti-racist policy and in ensuring same race placements for all children referred.

In recruiting a Black worker, several key issues were taken into account. Research and anecdotal evidence from throughout the UK suggests that:

- where Black workers are employed, they are usually on part-time, short-term or temporary contracts (Singh and Patel 1998)

- where Black workers are employed, they alone carry the full burden of the race equality remit

- unrealistic pressures are put on individual Black workers to achieve and perform against Eurocentric measures of outcome, without due regard to the assumptions inherent in such standards

- training and support, if provided at all, were usually reported as being inadequate.

Against this backdrop, it was important that any appointment of a Black worker should not be tokenistic, and should try to avoid these shortcomings, so that it did not perpetuate the very racism the project was attempting to combat. Thus, Barnardo's commitment to take on the funding of the post after the initial two years, was a strong statement of support and recognition of this need for proper status and permanence. It was also made explicit from the outset that the overall responsibility for the development of an anti-racist, same-race service within the project lay with the management structure and was not the sole remit of the Black worker. The success or failure of any recruitment campaign and subsequent development was seen as a team responsibility. In this way, the thinking and aspirations behind the post were shared and owned by the whole project.

A further recognition of the demands and nature of the post lay in its developmental role, which avoided unrealistic expectations about large numbers of carers being recruited over a short period of time. All family placement work is by its nature, slow and gradual. Recruiting and assessing Asian carers was seen in this context, where networking and information sharing are the crucial first, and often lengthy, steps. It is these foundations that have enabled the post to flourish and to become fully established. Out of this has developed a solid base of recruitment of Black and Asian carers, where, as with white applicants, it is the word of mouth and personal connections that produce a steady source of enquiries and thus resources for children (see Appendix 1 for more details).

DOING THE SAME – DIFFERENTLY

Clearly, anti-racist practice which attempts to tackle structural racism within systems to produce positive outcomes for children, does not happen overnight and is best seen as part of a process. We have identified below some of the key areas of work that we undertook in the first few years of the development of the Khandan Initiative, and would emphasise that this is an ongoing piece of development which includes a strategic review and evaluation process to enable us to maximise our learning, much of which has been a combination of 'try it and see' coupled with 'what's the theory?' and 'how have others done it?' A detailed account of the first year of the Khandan Initiative is given in a Barnardo's Scotland publication (1999) 'In on the Act'. Table 1 provides a summary of the key areas of practice and policy development that have enabled the Khandan Initiative to become established.

Table I. Key areas of practice and policy development

RECRUITING BLACK FAMILIES

Networking
– Initially made contact with relevant Black Asian Community Groups.
– Sought representation on appropriate groups, e.g. Scottish Anti-Racist Federation
– Promoted services with relevant professionals.
– Sought opportunities for face-to-face contact with interested parties.

Resources
– Project information translated into minority ethnic community languages e.g. Urdu, Punjabi, and Hindi.
– Use of interpreting and translating services.

ENQUIRIES AND INITIAL VISITS
– Nurturing approach to enquiries, with follow-up phone-calls by a bilingual worker, if required.
– Giving people space, time, support and information to enable them to give fostering and adoption their full consideration, as they may not have had access to full information within their own community and may not make use of white media in which these subjects are explored.
– All initial visits at the enquirer's home so that they could feel most comfortable.
– Monitoring system established for all enquirers to record their ethnic group and languages spoken.

PREPARATION AND TRAINING
– Decision taken that Black applicants should participate in preparation and training for Black families only; this was to ensure that applicants would not experience racism within a predominately white group and that shared experience of ethnicity and culture could be explored.
– Initially, because of small numbers, preparation and training was carried out with individual families as part of the assessment process. As numbers increased we were able to begin groups for Black applicants. These groups were facilitated in the group's first language by an interpreter and utilised social time so that people could put each other into the context of their own community; they specifically looked at the needs of Black children in placement.

ASSESSMENT
– Workers required to be open to the diversity and uniqueness of family systems. We cannot assume a homogenous group based on assumptions about Black and Asian cultures and beliefs. Assessment needed to explore family support systems and relationships.
– For applicants where English is a second language, workers have needed to ensure that thoughts and feelings could be expressed adequately. To be most effective an interpreter or bilingual worker should be utilised.

ADOPTION AND FOSTERING PANEL

- Panel members received training from a Black trainer, which focused on anti-racist practice and issues that could emerge in assessing Black families.
- Black panel members were recruited to provide balance in the panel and consultancy within the panel forum.
- Interpreters are used when required.

SUPPORT

- Support is provided according to each family's needs. There is recognition of the distinct roles of males and females in some families; workers of both genders need to be involved, with the female worker providing the main placement support to the woman and the male worker coming into periodic joint meetings with both carers.
- Involving male carers can be challenging, as many work long hours within Scottish Asian communities and time for religious practice is also paramount. It can be difficult at times to find space to meet with social workers, and the female carer tends to undertake the majority of the caring role.
- Support by a white worker may require the use of an interpreter, or support can be given by a bilingual worker.
- We are not yet at the stage of being able to provide support groups to Black families, but hope to in the future when we have a suitable number of families approved.

As Table 1 illustrates, the recruitment of Black families has been established and Family Placement Services is now placing Black children for adoption, fostering and respite care. Our next challenge is to explore ways of supporting families in the context of family patterns and community, which in some cases may be very different to the way in which white families are organised and supported by the Project.

CONCLUSION

There has been a long history, in Scotland at least, of services for Black children being planned on the basis of numbers rather than need. This approach, although financially effective for resource holders, has done little to address the inherent disadvantages in services to Black children, who are, in this context, low in numbers but who have significant and particular needs.

We welcome recent legislation in the form of the Children (Scotland) Act (1995), which has placed in statute the requirement that regard is given to every child's racial origin, religious persuasion, cultural and linguistic background. This is significant in placing the needs of Black children alongside the project principle of child welfare. The Macpherson Report (1999) places the responsibility on every institution to examine policy and practice to guard against disadvantaging any section of the community.

6

We hope that the outcome of this is that individual anti-racist practitioners no longer have to justify the 'need' for same-race placements for Black children. Statute and research evidences the clear priority that should be given to developing these services. Inaction by policy makers and budget holders can and should be questioned and examined in the context of structural and institutional racism. A commitment to take forward the ideas of the Act should be supported by social work managers and practitioners alike.

The Khandan Initiative provides an example of how an agency can take on the commitment to providing services to Black children, to tackling individual, structural and institutional racism and not polarising individual professionals. We have demonstrated that there are ways in which an agency can develop services that meet the needs of ALL children requiring family placement services in Scotland, and much of the learning would be transferable to developing a diverse range of services to Black children in areas where the actual populations may be small.

We have learned that in the area of adoption and fostering, attachment theory has been dominant and does offer much to our understanding of bonding, separation and loss, and re-parenting of children with substitute families. Black children need us to look beyond these theoretical ideas based in Euro-Centric thinking and the nuclear family and to consider the idea of extended family and community taking on a greater significance. We need to consider an understanding of identity incorporating a 'We' as much as an 'I'.

Current research evidence highlighting the concept of resilience has great potential in its application to Black children. It recognises the importance of primary attachment figures, but also highlights the benefit to the child of social relationships and resources beyond the nuclear family. This research takes account of cultural and social needs in the healthy development of identity and self-esteem in the child.

Theory and legislation alone will not promote change in practice. Change requires sound financial investment alongside a commitment to anti-racist practice and a belief in the rights of Black children to same-race placements.

What is required is:

> *dispassionate determination to use legislation ... and a passionate personal commitment to challenge racism wherever it exists.* (Scottish Office, 1998)

Appendix 1

During the first twelve months of the Khandan Initiative we received a total of 27 enquiries; these can be broken down as follows:

Pakistani Muslim	18
Indian Sikh	2
Indian Hindu	2
Mixed race couples	3
Other	2
TOTAL	27

Befrienders	4
Respite care	5
Short-term fostering	6
Permanent fostering	4
Adoption	8
TOTAL	27

In the second and third year of the Initiative we received a further 70 enquiries, and now continue to receive on average one or two enquiries a month.

We now have a number of families approved and children placed, as follows:

- three approved adoptive families. One of these has been approved twice and now has three children placed with them. Another of these has one child placed and is being matched for a second child, and the third is being matched with their first child

  one permanent foster family which has been approved to foster primary school children but is still waiting to be matched with children

- two families approved as respite carers; one of these has offered befriending to transracially placed children, and has more recently been providing respite for a number of white children.

REFERENCES

ABSWAP (1983) *Black Children in Care: Guidance to the House of Commons Social Services Committee*, ABSWAP.

Ainsworth M. et al. (1978) *Patterns of Attachment*, Lawrence Erlbaum.

Banks J. A. (1997) *Educating Citizens in a Multicultural Society*, Teachers College Press.

Barn R. (1993) *Black Children in the Public Care System*, Batsford Academic.

Barnardo's Scotland (1999) *In on the Act,*. Barnardo's, Edinburgh.

BEMIS (1999) *Listening to the Voice*, SCVO, Glasgow.

Bowes A. and Sim D. (eds) (1991) *Demands and Constraints: Ethnic Minorities and Social Services in Scotland*, SCVO, Edinburgh.

Bowlby J. (1969) *Attachment and Loss:* Vol. 1: Attachment, Hogarth Press, London.

Cadman M. and Chakrabarti M. (1991) 'Social work in a multi-racial society: a survey of practice in two Scottish Local Authorities'; in CCETSW, *One Small Step towards Racial Justice*, CCETSW, London.

Chahal K. and Julienne Z. (1999) *We Can't All be White!* York Publishing Services, York.

Cohen P. and Bains H.S. (eds) (1988) *Multi-Racist Britain*, Macmillan, Basingstoke.

Cooley C. H. (1902) *Human Nature and the Social Order*, Scribner's, New York.

Daniel B., Wassell S., and Gilligan R. (1999) '"It's just common sense isn't it"? Ways of putting the theory of resilience into action'. *Adoption and Fostering*, **23**(3), pp5-16

Divine D. (1983) 'Time for decision' in *The Caribbean Times* 18th March.

Dominelli L. (1998) *Anti Racist Social Work*, 2nd Ed. Macmillan, Basingstoke.

Fahlberg V. (1981) *Attachment and Separation*, BAAF, London.

Gambe D., Gomes J., Kapur M., Rangel P. and Stubb S. (1992) *Improving Practice with Children and Family: A Training Manual*, CCETSW, Nothern Curriculum Development Project.

Germaine G.B. (1979). 'Social work practice: people and environment', Maluccio A.N., Fein E. and Olmstead K.A. (1986) *Permanency Planning for Children: Concepts and Methods*, Tavistock.

Gilligan R. (1997) 'Beyond permanence: the importance of resilience in child placement practice and planning', *Adoption and Fostering* **21**(1), pp12-20.

Gilroy P. (1987) *Problems in Anti-racist Strategy*, Runnymede Trust

Great Britain (1995) The Children (Scotland) Act, HMSO , London.

Howe D. (1995) *Attachment Theory for Social Work Practice*, Macmillan, London.

Howe R. (1995). 'Redefining the transracial adoption controversy', *Duke Journal of Gender Law and Policy*, **2**(1), pp131.

Macpherson W. (1999) *The Stephen Lawrence Inquiry*, The Stationery Office, London.

McCluskey J. (1991) 'Ethnic minorities and the social work service in Glasgow', in Bowes A. and Sim D. (eds) (1991) *Demands and Constraints: Ethnic Minorities and Social Services in Scotland*, SCVO, Edinburgh.

McRoy J. (1991) 'Significance of ethnic and racial identity in intercountry adoption within the United States', *Journal of Adoption and Fostering*, **15**(4), pp53-61.

Mead G.H. (1934) Mind, Self and Society, From the Standpoint of a Social Behaviourist, University of Chicago Press, Chicago.

Nobles W. (1973) 'Psychological research and the Black self concept: a critical review', *Journal of Social Issues*, **29**(1), pp11-31.

Noble W. (1978) 'Towards an empirical and theoretical framework for defining Black families, *Journal of Marriage and the Family*, **70**, pp679-88.

OPCS (1993) Census. 1991, Part I, Vol. 1, HMSO, London.

Owusu-Bempah J. and Howitt D. (1997) 'Socio-genealogical connectedness, attachment theory and childcare practice', *Child and Family Social Work* **2**(4), pp199-207.

Robinson C. and West J. (1999) *Black Perspectives on Direct Practice in Social Work Training*. Caledonian University, Glasgow.

Scottish Office (1997) *The Children (Scotland) Act 1995: Regulations and Guidance: Vol 2: Children Looked After by Local Authorities*, The Stationery Office, Edinburgh.

The Scottish Office (1998) *Valuing Diversity*, The Stationery Office, Edinburgh.

Singh S. (1997) 'Assessing Asian families in Scotland: a discussion', *Adoption and Fostering*, **21**(3), pp35-39.

Singh S and Patel V.K.P. (1998) *Regarding Scotland's Black Children*, Scottish Black Workers Forum, Edinburgh.

Singh S., Patel V. and Falconer P. (2000) 'Confusion and perceptions: social work conceptions regarding Black children in Scotland', *Child Welfare Policy and Practice*, Hill, M and Iwaniec D. (eds) Jessica Kingsley, London.

Skellington R. and Morris P. (1992) *Race in Britain Today*, Sage, York.

Smith P. and Berridge D. (1993) *Ethnicity and Childcare Placements*, National Children's Bureau, London.

Tizzard B. and Phoenix A. (1993) *Black, White or Mixed Race?* Routledge, London and New York.

Wilson M. (1991) 'Beyond rhetoric', *Social Work Today* **22**(36) pp15-17.

World Health Organisation (1992) The ICD-10 *Classification of Mental and Behavioural Disorders: Clinical Descriptions and Diagnostic Guidelines*. WHO, Geneva.

Conclusion 7

Anne van Meeuwen

This publication has used selected examples of Barnardo's work with Black and South Asian communities to highlight some key points about policy and practice. It does not attempt to do justice to the full spectrum of our work with a range of diverse communities. The examples that are provided include both well-established areas of the organisation's work such as family placement and more recently identified issues such as the position of young carers. Some projects are located in areas where there is a long tradition of 'racial' and cultural diversity and others have been developing their practice in a context where until recently minority ethnic children have tended to be 'invisible'. However, despite the different content and contexts of the services illustrated, some common themes and transferable learning points do emerge.

None of the services would wish to claim that they have discovered the final answer to working appropriately with the communities they serve or indeed that such an answer exists. Rather, they are engaged in a process, a journey on which the terrain, the routes and the possible destination may often shift or become contested, but along which tips may be gathered which can usefully be shared with other travellers. At times, internal or external factors may require parts of this journey to be revisited, hopefully informed by what has been learnt in the interim. An example of this would be the debate around the placement of children in 'racially' and culturally appropriate families. The arguments that led to the development of same-race placement policies in the 1980s have had to be re-visited, particularly in adoption, in the face of political and media criticism of alleged 'political correctness'. Hopefully such arguments can now be informed by both a more sophisticated understanding of identity issues and practical experience of what works in recruiting minority ethnic families.

Before moving on to identify what themes and learning points can be extracted from the case studies, it may be helpful to locate these within current debates both in the wider context and more specifically in social care for children and families. The Children Act 1989 and the Children (Scotland) Act 1995 require consideration of a child's racial, cultural, religious and linguistic background, and whilst the legislation relates to the decision-making process for looked after children, in practice such a requirement would be regarded as equally pertinent to services for children in need. However, several years after the implementation of the 1989 Act, a recent SSI report *Excellence not Excuses* (O'Neale, 2000) has identified how much more needs to be achieved in order to make a positive difference to the lives of minority ethnic children and their families. Specific areas of concern include:

- little evidence of the implementation of equality policies

- the lack of a robust response to instances of abuse and harassment

- responding to the support and development needs of minority ethnic staff

- a lack of staff understanding about the situation of black families.

Barn (1999) has noted the lack of 'an adequate conceptual framework, ... that could and should encompass issues of "race and ethnicity". In her view such a framework raises questions about how we perceive the nature and dynamics of culture and understand the impact of racism on families and communities and about how such perceptions and understanding inform our policy and practice. This reflects wider debates outside the field of social care. Writing about the emergence of 'new ethnicities', Hall (1992) refers to 'recognition of immense diversity and differentiation in the historical and cultural experiences of black subjects', and in attempting to define the concept of ethnicity states 'we all speak from a particular place, out of a particular history, a particular culture'. In his view the commonality of the experience of racism will be filtered through various prisms such as class, gender and sexuality – we could add disability and age. This suggests that the starting point needs to be the meaning of the experience for the individual and a contextual understanding of how they might choose to respond. For Hall, the emergence of 'new ethnicities' is part of a contested discourse about what it means to be British. This has been developed further in the report of the Commission on the Future of Multi-Ethnic Britain (2000). The Commission's vision is of a Britain which is a 'Community of Communities' with seven fundamental principles informing the way ahead:

- three central concepts: equality, diversity and cohesion

- demonstrable change at all levels

- addressing racism

- tackling disadvantage

- colour-blind approaches do not work

- empowering and enfranchising

- a pluralistic culture of human rights.

In the view of the Commission, the present Government's modernising and social exclusion agendas have been characterised by a colour- and culture-blind approach. The invisibility of minority ethnic children within the original objectives of the Quality Protects, programme published in September 1998, would be a good example of this. However, since late 1999, possibility as a result of the Macpherson report, there has been a definite shift, with a number of more positive initiatives, such as the inclusion of the Commission for Racial Equality standards in the Best Value regime. A continuing area of concern is the emphasis on time-limited, project-based funding streams which may encourage the development of specific short-term initiatives for minority ethnic children. However if core funding is not available, their access to mainstream services in the longer term may not be significantly improved.

So within the context of a wider debate that emphasises the recognition and valuing of cultural diversity alongside the need to tackle racism, inequality and disadvantage, what are the lessons emerging from practice?

■ the importance of starting from where people are – not making assumptions, not relying on stereotypes, but finding out about the issues of 'race' and culture that are important to that individual, that family, that community and about the meanings they attach to them. Such an approach may involve a radical re-think of how a service is delivered rather than the adaptation of tried and tested models which have developed from a Eurocentric perspective and which may only be suited to the needs of members of the indigenous community

■ respecting and validating what people have to offer – drawing on strengths, seeing the community as a resource, complementing rather than replacing what members of minority ethnic communities are already doing to address an issue and working in collaboration with organisations in the Black voluntary sector. For some projects, the most effective interventions may be in the fields of capacity building and tackling the structural barriers which prevent families from accessing resources

■ establishing trust and credibility – being reliable, demonstrating integrity, observing confidentiality and again treating people with respect. In addition to the qualitative aspects of interpersonal relationships, giving time and attention to concrete practical actions and delivering the service promised is likely to be more effective than any number of eloquent policy statements

■ open and clear communication – informing people about the services available, listening to their views, addressing areas of concern. The impact of racism undermines any belief children and families may have in being listened to, having their views taken seriously and their concerns addressed. By modelling

best practice in this area, service providers can go some way towards
suggesting that an alternative approach is possible

■   enabling people to feel comfortable – communicating in different languages,
    and looking at the composition of the staff group, the physical environment
    and the location of the project

■   being responsive and flexible about service delivery – being willing to learn,
    review, adapt and again to listen

■   commitment and ownership by the project as a whole – clear policies, training,
    supervision and staff support systems. The extent to which the services
    described are delivered by minority ethnic staff varies. However, the
    importance of a shared commitment by all staff cannot be underestimated.

The above points have emerged directly from the practice experience of projects on
the ground, but such projects do not operate in a vacuum. Clearly their ability to
deliver a service which is consistent with good practice principles will be affected by
their organisational and external context. Organisational systems, policies, resourcing
and perhaps more importantly culture can either support or undermine the efforts of
practitioners and frontline managers to work appropriately and effectively with
children and families from minority ethnic communities. Where an organisation has
developed specific initiatives to meet the needs of particular communities, it is vital
that these are not just short-term initiatives and a strategy is developed to sustain the
service in the longer term through mainstream service provision. Equally the existence
of such initiatives should not divert attention from the need to ensure that all of an
organisation's services are accessible, flexible and responsive to the needs of children
and families from minority ethnic communities. Gilroy has written of the tendency of
racialised discourses to construct minority ethnic subjects as either 'problems' or
'victims' (Gilroy, 1987). Political and media debate concerning refugee and asylum
seekers has reinforced the continued potency of such discourse. Within the field of
social care, the difficulties that organisations face in responding appropriately to the
needs of some children and families may be articulated, albeit less overtly, through
similar discourse. We need a new discourse within which minority ethnic children and
families are construed as citizens, entitled to services which are relevant to what they
perceive to be their needs. What is striking about many of the above practice points is
their relevance to work with all children, all families and communities – recognition,
respect, trust and honesty are important to everybody. This is not about being colour-
or culture-blind, but perhaps if organisations really do start from where people are,
value and respect them as citizens and hear what they have to say, what emerges are
ways to make a difference to children and families as rich and diverse as the
communities they represent.

REFERENCES

7

Barn R. (ed.) (1999) *Working with Black Children and Adolescents in Need*, British Agencies for Adoption and Fostering, London.

Commission on the Future of Multi-ethnic Britain (2000) *The Future of Multi-ethnic Britain*, Profile Books, London (The Parekh Report).

Gilroy P. (1987) *There Ain't no Black in the Union Jack*, Hutchinson, London.

Hall S. (1992) 'New ethnicities', in Donald J. and Rattansi A. (eds) *'Race', Culture and Difference*, Sage and Open University.

Macpherson W. (1999) *The Stephen Lawrence Inquiry*, The Stationery Office, London.

O'Neale V. (2000) *Excellence not Excuses: Inspection of Services for Ethnic Minority Children and Families*. Department of Health, London

HAVERING COLLEGE OF F & H E

39098